Fourteen Presidents
Before Washington

Fourteen Presidents Before Washington

THE AMERICAN HISTORY
YOU NEVER LEARNED IN SCHOOL

Herman D. Hover

DODD, MEAD & COMPANY

NEW YORK

Published by Dodd, Mead & Company, Inc.
79 Madison Avenue, New York, N.Y. 10016
Distributed in Canada by
McClelland and Stewart Limited, Toronto
Manufactured in the United States of America
First Edition

Library of Congress Cataloging in Publication Data

Hover, Herman D.
   Fourteen presidents before Washington.

   1. United States—History—Miscellanea.   I. Title.
E179.H84   1984   973   83-16403
ISBN 0-396-08229-7 (pbk.)

TO IAN, RENEE, & NICHOLAS

& MY BELOVED DAUGHTER ELLEN (1953-1977)

CONTENTS

1
The
New World

SHOULD WE ABOLISH Columbus Day, the national holiday celebrated each year on October 12? Columbus never set foot on the North American continent, and the door to the American mainland had been opened long before 1492. As early as 300 B.C. the Greeks envisioned a world beyond the western sea. Chinese scholars contend that nine hundred years before Columbus, Buddhist seamen had explored what is now California and Mexico. Land-hungry Vikings came to Iceland in A.D. 874 and Greenland in A.D. 986. And scholars believe that Africans visited the New World around the year A.D. 1000.

Eric the Red led his band of Icelandic Vikings westward to the unknown shores of Greenland, but he was not seeking new land. He was fleeing from Iceland where he had been sentenced to three years in exile for having participated in a bloody feud, a sentence that under Icelandic law made him fair game for anyone to kill.

On August 2, 1492, the last of the Jews fled Spain. On August 3, Columbus weighed anchor and set sail. Queen Isabella said she would pawn her jewels to pay for the voyage, but when she and King Ferdinand gave Christopher Columbus the money to go on his quest for a new route to the Indies, Isabella didn't have to pawn the jewels. The king and queen helped finance the unknown Genoese mariner on the expedition that led to the discovery of the greatest secret in history with money they confiscated from Spanish Jews.

The financial backing was meager. Columbus was given three small ships weighing a total of 190 tons, and his crew consisted mainly of convicts released from prison on the condition that they make the trip. The entire expedition cost somewhere between fifteen and twenty thousand dollars, not a very generous sum even in those days.

Five *Marranos* shipped with Columbus. The *Marranos* were Jews who accepted baptism to escape the Inquisition's pyre. Columbus's Jews were able seamen Alonzo de la Calle; fleet surgeon, Senor Marco; fleet physician, Senor Blanco; Roderigo Sanches, who represented Queen Isabella and was the nephew of Gabriel Sanches, a benefactor of the voyage; and Louis Vaer de Torres, a scholar and interpreter who knew the customs and languages of the Far East.

Columbus did not go on his voyage of discovery directly, but stopped off at the Canary Islands. In Las Palmas, on Grand Canary Island, you can visit the lovely old house where the admiral stayed while his ships reprovisioned and his men rested before leaving on their great Atlantic crossing.

On his first visit to the Western world, Columbus came across a unique type of bed used by the Caribbean natives. It consisted of interlaced creepers and they called it a *hammock*. The admiral conceived it would be ideal aboard ship, where space was limited and the motion frequently turbulent.

The island where Columbus first touched land in the New World is named after an English pirate. Exactly where Columbus landed on October 12, 1492, and planted a cross in thanksgiving for a safe journey is not agreed upon among scholars, but San Salvador, known today as Watling's Island for the English buccaneer, John Watling, is favored.

Although Columbus and his crew set sail on the maiden voyage to the New World in a caravan of three ships, they returned to Spain with only two. The flagship *Santa Maria* was stranded on a reef near Cap-Haïtien in Haiti and was abandoned, with the admiral transferring his flag to the tiny *Nina*. Timbers of the wreck were used to build Fort Navidad. Columbus left forty men at the fort and arrived in Lisbon on March 4, 1493, with a few copper-skinned aborigines, some gold dust, and samplings of New World flora. The admiral spun tales of an exotic realm of gold and pearls, strange herbs and fruits, and even stranger natives who went about "as naked as when their mothers bore them."

"Aha, Indians!" cried Christopher Columbus when he landed, smacking his lips like an Italian gourmet who has just sampled his own spaghetti sauce. Columbus called the friendly natives "Indians" and believed all the rest of his life that the islands he had found were part of the Indies.

Oranges are not indigenous to Florida or California, but were brought to the New World by Columbus. Every Spanish sailor who went to the New World was required by law to take with him no fewer than one hundred orange seeds.

Much of the documentation covering Christopher Columbus's early life is suspect in one way or another, but it is now generally agreed that this Spanish-speaking navigator was born in Genoa. The great admiral's end was almost as obscure as his beginnings. Even his burial place has been a matter of dispute, with both the cathedrals of Santo Domingo in the West Indies and Seville in Spain claiming to hold his remains.

"Christopher Columbus" is alive and well and living in Madrid. A direct descendant of Columbus, nineteen generations removed, one of Spain's most titled men, is Duke de Vergia, Marquis of Jamaica, Viceroy of the Indies, Admiral of the Ocean Sea, twice a Grandee, and a lieutenant commander in the Spanish Navy.

Curiously, the first voyages to the New World undertaken by Spain, Britain, and France were under the command of Italian navigators. John Cabot, who first planted the British flag in America, was born Giovanni Cabato, and like Columbus who sailed under the Spanish flag, was Genoese. Giovanni da Verrazano, who explored the New York harbor eighty-five years before Henry Hudson, was Florentine, but sailed for France. The co-founder of Detroit and its commander for ten years was Alfonso Tonti, whose daughter was the first white child born there. Moreover, eight of the priests who founded Spanish missions in California were Italian.

The first man to sail around the world was Sebastian del Cano. Ferdinand Magellan, a Portuguese navigator in the service of Spain, had set out in August 1519 with five rickety ships to reach the Indies by sailing westward, but was killed in the Philippine Islands. Del Cano completed Magellan's task.

Spanish culture in the New World followed fast upon the heels of conquest. The first printing press was set up in New Spain in 1539, and both Mexico City and Lima—the "City of Kings"—became seats of learning within fifteen years of the conquest; in each, a university was founded in 1551. Thus, the Spanish empire in America had more than a century's head start on the Empires of England and France.

Normally inhospitable to foreigners, the government of Spain welcomed Irishmen into its New World service as Roman Catholics and enemies of England. Some of these Hispanicized Hibernians went far. One of them, O'Donoju, was the last viceroy of Mexico. A contemporary, Carlos Murfi, was the last royal governor of Paraguay. Another, O'Reilly, was governor of Cuba and Louisiana.

Ambrose Higgins came an impoverished immigrant from County Heath to Spain, where he affixed the aristocratic Irish "O" to his name. In his days of glory he ascended to become captain-general of Chile and, finally, viceroy of Peru and a marquis in the peerage of Spain. In

[7]

the New World no Spaniard could go higher.

In his ventures O'Higgins sired a son, Bernardo, born a Chilean and—ironically—destined to lead his people's struggle for independence from the nation his father had served so loyally. When Chile became a free country, Bernardo O'Higgins was to be its first presidente. Today the name O'Higgins is seen everywhere: countless plazas, streets, and hotels bear it proudly.

By the time European colonists first arrived in the New World, Indians were harvesting the greatest variety of vegetables, fruits, and other crops that had ever been known. Among the species grown were corn (called by the Indians *maize*), cashew nuts, vanilla beans, tobacco, rubber, coca (for cocaine), cinchona (from which they extracted quinine), several varieties of cotton, pumpkins, cacao (for chocolate), pineapples, peanuts, potatoes, and tomatoes. Their domestic animals were dogs, turkeys, guinea pigs, and in some areas llamas.

Giovanni Cabato, the Italian navigator whom the English called John Cabot, set sail from Bristol in 1497. He landed in what is today Canada, claimed the land for England, and returned home, where King Henry VII gave him ten pounds sterling with which "to have a good time" and a pension of twenty pounds a year.

Cabot was the first European to land on the North American mainland. His discoveries were the basis for England's eventual claim to the whole of North America. As Cabot sailed up and down the northern Atlantic coast of the New World he described the land as a new-found land, which today survives in the name Newfoundland.

Englishmen took it for granted that the red men of America were one of the ten lost tribes of Israel mentioned in the Bible.

When the people of Europe heard of such strange New World creatures as bison, raccoon, and opossum, they at first imagined these animals to be mythical beasts like unicorns and dragons.

Hernando Cortés, the lawyer from Salamanca who conquered the Aztecs and plundered the gold of Mexico, also introduced chocolate to Europe by bringing the original recipe for *chocolatl* from the Aztec court. A dark, bitter drink that had to be tempered with sugar and milk before it was palatable, *chocolatl* was taken for granted as an aphrodisiac, and Montezuma II always fortified himself with a goodly amount of the liquid when he walked into his harem, in the belief that it would reinvigorate him.

When Cortés invaded Mexico, the Indians had never before seen horses and thought that the horse and rider, both arrayed in spangled armor, were some thunderous new, godlike creature. Cortés, aware of their astonishment, never allowed horses killed in battle to remain on the battlefield, but secretly had them buried so that the Indians would believe they were impervious to injury.

At the time the Europeans first landed in Mexico, in 1519, they found a native civilization that surpassed their own in many ways. Not only was the Indian capital Tenochtitlan, today known as Mexico City, larger than Rome or Paris was then, but the Indians' calendar was more accurate than the European calendar and their system of sanitation was superior. In fact, the Indians thought that the Europeans smelled bad.

Although the Incas had no written language, they managed their empire so well that no one went hungry or cold.

Peter Minuit, the Dutch colonial official who founded what is now New York, bought Manhattan Island from its Indian proprietors for sixty guilders worth of trinkets, gewgaws, notions, and sundries, give or take a bead. Somebody a long time later translated that into twenty-four dollars.

Minuit pulled off an even slicker deal than the legendary purchase of Manhattan. The Dutch administrator was a masterful supersalesman. Watching him was like watching a chess expert. He was always two or three moves ahead of you. In exchange for a few trinkets and some potent Swedish "firewater," he smooth-talked the local Indian chiefs into ceding the Dutch all of the land on both sides of the Delaware River, extending to "where the sun sets." However, he was bested by the Raritan Indians—real wheeler-dealers who sold Staten Island to the Dutch six successive times.

Sir Francis Drake landed in the San Francisco area in 1579 and named all of California "New Albion," claiming it for England. Drake returned to England in 1588, wealthy with booty plundered from Spanish merchant-men and soon to be knighted by Queen Elizabeth I.

In 1611, Henry Hudson, who explored what are now the Hudson River, the Hudson Straits, and Hudson's Bay for the British, was set adrift by his mutinous crew in a small boat in Hudson's Bay and never heard from again.

When Henry Hudson sailed his eighty-ton ship the *Half Moon* into lower New York Bay in 1609, he had already been preceded by the sixteenth-century Italian navigator and explorer Giovanni da Verrazano, who was actually the first European to discover the Hudson River.

Da Verrazano made his claim to greatness as an explorer only after first being a pirate. He had captured two ships dispatched by Cortés from Mexico, and the booty so impressed King Francis I of France, who had commissioned Verrazano, that the King asked him to further explore the coast of the New World with a view to French settlement and to be on the alert for the capture of more treasure ships.

The potato is not indigenous to Ireland. Sir Walter Raleigh brought it there from North Carolina in the 1550s.

Tobacco, the bewitching weed smoked by the Indians, was another product brought by Raleigh from the New World to the Old, where it became a fashionable habit with the Europeans. When Raleigh's servant first saw him smoking, however, he poured water over his master, thinking that he was on fire.

Portuguese explorers of the New World would bring along convicts and cast them ashore in unknown areas to find out whether the natives were cannibals.

Slavery existed in South America even before North America, but with these significant differences: In North America slaves lived at a bare subsistence level; the enslaved were mere chattels, bought and sold as such. In South America a slave was treated as a person, not an object. Marriage was a sacred rite and the Latin American slave could be a husband and a father, merchant, or artisan, and could even become a priest or military officer. Never did his master have the power of life and death over him. Finally, there were no color barriers; once freed, a black slave was accepted on equal terms with white freemen.

The first Africans came to the New World not in bondage but accompanying the European explorers. Pedro Alonso Niño, one of Columbus's pilots and remembered among the great navigators of the sea, was a black African. When Balboa discovered the Pacific Ocean in 1513, thirty black men were in his party. Esteban, a florid and illiterate black giant, opened up to European settlers the rich area that is now Arizona and New Mexico.

In the middle of the fifteenth century, the Portuguese were exploring the west coast of Africa, where they bar-

tered with the native population not only for gold and
ivory, but for tribesmen the natives had captured in inter-
tribal wars. Neither of the parties considered selling and
bartering humans as wrongful. That was how enslave-
ment of blacks originated and it was to continue for four
centuries, the United States being the last nation to give
it up.

Fate has not been kind to seekers and discoverers. Magellan was killed before completing his voyage; Columbus
and Cortés died in poverty, litigating against rivals;
Pizarro was assassinated; Hudson fell victim to muti-
neers; Sir Francis Drake died of fever on an expedition;
Captain James Cook was eaten by cannibalistic islanders;
and Sir Walter Raleigh was beheaded on trumped-up
charges.

2
Early
Americans

WHEN THE *MAYFLOWER* finally set sail on September 16, 1620, only fifty-one passengers on board were Pilgrims. They called themselves "Saints." The fifty non-Pilgrims were called "Strangers" and included "goodmen" (they were the ordinary settlers), ten indentured servants, one professional soldier, and four little London orphans bound out to labor without wages until they should be twenty-one years old. Among the "Strangers" was a powerfully built young cooper by the name of John Alden, who, speaking for himself, would marry Priscilla Mullins in the marriage romanticized by Henry Wadsworth Longfellow. Also among the passengers were some intractables, one of whom, John Billington, was ultimately hanged for murder.

The Pilgrims were not Puritans but Separatists. The Puritans, another group, did not find it necessary to leave England in order to worship in peace.

The *Mayflower* was a rather old freighter that had never before carried passengers, and its name was a very common one: at least twenty *Mayflowers* are recorded in the port records of the era.

After its voyage to the New World, the *Mayflower* was returned to England, where it was dismantled in 1624. The timber was used to build a barn.

By the end of their first winter in their new homeland, more than half of the Pilgrims had died. Even so, when the *Mayflower* set sail in the spring to return to England, none of the survivors chose to return.

In colonial times both men and women had strong body odors. They seldom bathed, considering it unhealthy, which it probably was in the severe New England winters.

Wives were considered chattels and could be dealt with as such. Husbands hired them out as domestics and pocketed their wages, and if a wife ran away she might properly be accused of stealing herself and the clothing she was wearing, since both were owned by the husband.

Bundling was, by the end of the 1700s, an accepted part of courtship in the American Colonies. In this practice, the couple would spend the night together in the girl's bed, both fully dressed. A center board theoretically separated them. In certain churches, approval of a marriage was contingent on a full confession of sins by the bride and groom; the records of one church show that almost half

the couples making such confessions admitted carnal
knowledge of each other.

"Witches" were not burned at the stake in Salem. Although nearly 150 men and women were arrested, only
19 were found guilty, and they were hanged.

Thanksgiving Day originated in Holland in 1574. The
Netherlands was at war with Spain, and the people of
Leiden, which was under siege, held off the enemy for 131
days. Their food was exhausted and six thousand died of
starvation and fever, but the Dutch threw off the yoke of
Spanish imperialism on October 3, and King William the
Silent was so grateful that he offered the citizens of Leiden
either perpetual freedom from taxation or a university.
They chose the university, and a celebration has been held
on October 3 every year since. The Pilgrims spent twelve
years in Leiden, and by the time they arrived at Plymouth
had experienced many Thanksgivings.

One of the first settlers of the Plymouth Colony was
Abraham Pearce, a black man. Pearce was not there as a
slave; although he had originally joined the Colony as an
indentured servant in 1623, he owned land, voted, and
had equal standing in the community—which was
spelled *Plimoth* at the time. The presence of a black man
at Plymouth shatters the stereotype of the exclusively
European Pilgrim.

Virginia is often given the short end in history books. A
great deal has been written about the *Mayflower* but lit-

tle about the *Susan Constant,* the ship that landed the Jamestown settlers more than a dozen years before the *Mayflower* landed her shipload at Plymouth. In fact, Plymouth itself had been visited years before by Captain John Smith of the Virginia Colony, and it was Smith, not the Pilgrims, who named the place.

The Declaration of Independence was written by a Virginian, the first president of the United States was a Virginian, and of the first twelve presidents of the United States, seven were from Virginia. And while the whole of New England provided six presidents, Virginia alone has given us eight.

The mystery of what happened to the Roanoke Colony in Virginia has never been adequately explained. John White, governor of the colony, went back to England in 1587 for desperately needed supplies, but was delayed three years. When he finally sailed back into Roanoke Sound, the more than one hundred colonists were gone without a trace. Historians still do not know their fate. Some say the group was slaughtered by warring bands of Indians. Others say they moved south with friendly Indians and that the pale-skinned Lumbee Indians are descendants of the original settlers.

Virginia Dare, first native white American, was born in 1587. In all accuracy, she should rightfully have been named North Carolina Dare since she was born on Roanoke Island, which according to charts of the 1700s is on the eastern mainland of North Carolina. However, Queen Elizabeth, who proclaimed herself a virgin, was the financial backer and moral supporter of Sir Walter Raleigh, and he therefore named the new land Virginia in her honor. The Dares, thinking that that was where they were, christened their baby girl Virginia.

In colonial America, more than two hundred crimes were punishable by death.

One of the mysteries of colonial America is why, with a population less than half that of modern Los Angeles, it provided a galaxy of distinguished leaders—including Benjamin Franklin, George Washington, John Adams, Thomas Jefferson, Alexander Hamilton, James Madison, George Mason, and John Marshall—that we cannot begin to duplicate today.

3
The
Revolution

INDEPENDENCE DAY should be celebrated on July 2, the anniversary of Congress's adoption of the Resolution of Independence. On July 4, Congress merely adopted Jefferson's Declaration.

The Fourth of July is generally considered the day when the Declaration of Independence was signed. In fact only John Hancock, president of Congress, affixed his name that day, as a token signature to make the document official. Fifty-two more members of the Congress signed on August 2; the remaining three signed later—one of them, Thomas McKean of Delaware, in 1781. Henry Wisner, the only New Yorker who voted for the Declaration, missed his chance for immortality because he neglected to sign the document.

The Declaration was originally written in French. The first sheets, which have been seen by few Americans, are kept in a safe.*

* The Declaration of Independence displayed in a glass case in the Library of Congress is not Jefferson's original copy. The original sheets contain a clause denouncing the slave trade and slavery, which was knocked out by delegates from South Carolina and Georgia. Had the clause been allowed to stand it would have led to the abolition of slavery at that time and saved the tragic loss of life in the Civil War.

The adoption of the Declaration on July 4 went virtually unnoticed in England, where the ceremony received only a six-line mention in a London paper, buried below a theater review.

John Adams first named Jefferson to the Committee of Five that drafted the Declaration, then convinced him to do the actual writing. Here is the dialogue that Adams committed to his diary:

> Jefferson proposed to me to make the draft and I said, "I will not, you shall do it."
> "Oh no!"
> "Why will you not?"
> "I will not. You ought to do it."
> "I will not."
> "Why?"
> "Reasons enough."
> "What can be your reasons?"
> "Reason first, you are a Virginian and Virginia would have to appear to be at the head of this business. Reason second, I am obnoxious, suspected and unpopular; you are very much otherwise. Reason third, you can write ten times better than I."

George Washington never signed the Declaration. It was first publicly proclaimed on July 8, 1776, and read before Washington and his troops in New York, where the Commander in Chief was already fighting the War for Independence.

The Boston Massacre was not really a massacre. There were three dead and two wounded, and the British Redcoats who did the shooting were brought to trial, where John Adams defended them. The Redcoats were acquitted of murder, although two were convicted of a lesser offense for which they were lightly punished.

The English tea tax of 1773 had the same effect on the colonists as waving a red flag has on a bull. The outrage that it provoked led ultimately to the Boston Tea Party. Surprisingly, the tea tax was not imposed by England for revenue, but to maintain the principle that Parliament retained its right to tax the Colonies without their consent. By 1773, most of Parliament's taxes on the Colonies had already been repealed, and it was expected that the defiant colonists would be satisfied with the apparent victory and abandon their opposition to the levying of taxes by the mother country.

Haym Salomon, Polish-born banker and American colonial patriot, lent the Revolutionary government a total of seven hundred thousand dollars, without which the United States would probably still be part of Great Britain. The money consisted of Salomon's entire fortune, and provided 35 percent of the cost of the Revolutionary War. A note for the full amount was issued to Salomon on March 27, 1782, by Robert Morris, superintendent of finance for the Continental government, but was never paid, and Salomon died impoverished.

There are historians who say that Benedict Arnold— whose name is a symbol of perfidy—was an able general and patriotic in his motives; that he turned to the British because he was convinced that the Colonies, owing to the incompetence of the Continental Congress, would fall to France.

Because more than half of the thirty thousand German troops brought to America by the English were furnished by the Landgrave of Hesse-Cassel, the word *Hessian* came to be applied to all of the German mercenaries.

Frederick the Great was uncommonly impressed with George Washington's ability to turn strategic retreats into victories. He sent the American general a sword bearing the inscription: "From the oldest General in the world to the best."

The true full name of the French marquis who helped the ragtag American colonists win their independence was Jean Marie Paul Roche Yves Gilbert Motier, Marquis de LaFayette.

There never was a Battle of Bunker Hill. The battle was fought on Breed's Hill, which adjoins its better known neighbor. The British captured the Hill on the third assault.

At the "Battle of Bunker Hill" the American forces had virtually no gunpowder, and their commander, Colonel William Prescott, did not dare let any go to waste. Every bullet had to count. American troops had to allow the British to come within short range no matter how frightening it would be to untrained young farmers. Prescott's famous order, "Don't shoot until you see the whites of their eyes," was not so much for bravery as for the powder shortage.

Ethan Allen's Green Mountain Boys, who fought so valiantly during the Revolution, were originally recruited for the purpose of fighting off settlers who came to Vermont from New York.

"Had it not been for this infamous island, the American Revolution could not possibly have subsisted," said British Admiral George Brydges Rodney of the Caribbean island of Statia [pronounced Stay-shuh]. During the American Revolutionary War, vessels from Dutch-ruled Statia shuttled arms and supplies to the rebellious Colonies. On November 16, 1776, the armed North American brigantine *Andrea Doria*, flying the Great Union flag, dropped anchor in the harbor of the small island and was accorded an eleven-gun salute, the first formal acknowledgment of the sovereignty of the United States of America by a foreign power.

Dutch-ruled and known today as St. Eustatius the island glitters with bright feathered birds whose local names are as colorful as their plumage: Bananaquit, Kill-'em Polly, Sugarbird, Betsy-Kick-Up, Mary-Shake-Well, Crackpot Soldier, four o'clock bird, and the brown pelican with its beak holding more than its belican.

"I have not yet begun to fight" were the inspiring words of Captain John Paul Jones when asked to surrender his *Bonhomme Richard* in its famous battle with the British frigate *Serapis* under the command of Captain Richard

Pearson. But the British captain never heard Jones's courageous defiance and sank the American ship despite the bravado of its commander.

Jones, born in Scotland, was not a citizen of America and never commanded an American fleet, although he did become Commodore of the Russian Navy.

All that most people know about Paul Revere is his riding a horse and waking the countryside yelling, "The British are coming!" In fact, Revere never made the ride; it was made by William Dawes, who had been chosen in the first place to ride to Lexington to warn Samuel Adams and John Hancock of the British invasion. Revere left after Dawes had already started, in case Dawes should be captured. The two met at Lexington and together left for Concord, but when a British mounted patrol surprised them, Dawes put spurs to his horse and escaped, while the frustrated Revere was captured to be later thrust into immortality by the poet Longfellow's caprice.

Betsy Ross, the best known woman of the Revolutionary generation, is—like Paul Revere—known for something she did not do. The legend that she designed and made the first American flag has been discredited. Betsy was a seamstress who sewed Pennsylvania's state navy flags for gunboats on the Delaware River, and had nothing to do with the Stars and Stripes. The story that has been handed down relates that a committee of the Continental Congress, made up of George Washington, Robert Morris, and George Ross, was appointed to decide upon a flag for the new United States. The three are said to have agreed upon a sketch that featured six-pointed stars and to have then called upon Mrs. Ross and asked her to sew up a flag based on their design. Instead, goes the story, she induced them to substitute five-pointed stars by demonstrating how she could cut out such stars with one snip of the scissors. The first time anyone heard the tale about her was in 1870—93 years later, when it was mentioned in a speech made by her grandson before the Historical Society of Pennsylvania.

Historians have never yet agreed upon who designed and made the first American flag; however, Judge Francis Hopkinson, signer of the Declaration of Independence, poet, artist, pamphleteer, musician, and organist of Christ Church in Philadelphia, is respected by his contemporaries as having designed the Stars and Stripes in 1777.

The American flag had fifteen stripes from 1795 to 1818, when the number was reduced to thirteen by an Act of Congress.

Historical research has proved that Nathan Hale never said, "I only regret that I have but one life to lose for my country," and that Patrick Henry never said, "Give me liberty or give me death!"

Who wrote Patrick Henry's speech? William Wirt, a cultivated Virginia lawyer and man of letters, published a biography on Henry in 1817 and penned many of the words that made Patrick Henry famous. It was common for writers in Wirt's time to put speeches in the mouths of a historical figure—words that he might have said, or was reported to have said, or should have said, or possibly never said at all. Thus the ringing phrase "Give me liberty or give me death!" that became a rallying cry in the Revolution is more likely William Wirt's than Patrick Henry's.

Not all the British colonies in North America rebelled against England. Only thirteen fought in the Revolution. Nova Scotia, a fourteenth colony, was separated from the other colonies by a sea, and had no identity with the mainland warmongers. Canada, largely inhabited by French Catholics, preferred British rule to dominion by the Protestants of New England. The British West Indies, which consisted of two islands—Jamaica and Barbados— were also separated from the other colonies by a sea, and their white minorities feared that the much larger number of black slaves on the islands could not be held in subjugation if the revolt spread. The West Indies were far less troublesome to the British and more favorably regarded by the mother country than the mainland Colonies.

At the time of the Revolution, 50 percent of the people in the Colonies were slaves or indentured servants.

Blacks in colonial America were not all poverty-stricken slaves. Some were free and wealthy, and a number of black freemen not only owned slaves of their own, whom they imported from their native lands in Africa, but even brought in indentured servants from England. In 1670 the Virginia Assembly passed a law making it illegal for black freemen to own white servants.

George III, king of England during the Revolution, is portrayed in history texts as evil and moronic, but might have been considered a "good guy" in our own century. A popular monarch in Britain and the Colonies, he was conscientious, athletic, and led an impeccable private life.

Morocco was the first nation to recognize the fledgling American republic, in 1777, and has maintained unbroken and friendly relations with the United States for more than two centuries, adhering to the longest running treaty the United States has ever negotiated.

Who were the fifty-six men who were to become known as the Founding Fathers? They were ordinary, typical Americans—a mixture of native-born and foreign-born, some rich and many poor, farmers and mechanics, physicians and merchants, self-made and to-the-manner born. Numbering Protestants, Catholics, and Free-Thinkers, some had book learning and twenty-nine were college graduates. Their average age was forty-two. Actually, the fifty-six signers never met in one place at one time, and a few were not even involved in the crucial vote for independence on July 2, 1776.

4
The
New Nation

THERE WERE NINE original states, not thirteen. The Constitutional Congress provided that "Ratification of the convention by nine states shall be sufficient for the Establishment of this Constitution between the states so ratifying same." Delaware was the first state to ratify, on December 6, 1787. Pennsylvania and New Jersey also ratified that month. Three more—Georgia, Connecticut, and Massachusetts—were in by February 6, then came Maryland and South Carolina. The ninth state to ratify, New Hampshire, made the Constitution a reality on June 21, 1788.

The United States does not celebrate the birth of the Republic, which should be June 21.

We had fourteen presidents before George Washington. They were the presidents of the Continental Congress from 1774 to 1789, and their names were Peyton Randolph, Henry Middleton, John Hancock, Henry Laurens, John Jay, Samuel Huntington, Thomas McKean, John Hanson, Elias Boudinot, Thomas Mifflin, Richard Henry Lee, Nathan Gorham, Arthur St. Clair, and Cyrus Griffin.

John Hanson is considered by some to be the first United States president, since he was the first to serve under the Articles of Confederation. His term of office ran from November 5, 1781 to November 4, 1782.

The expiring Congress of the Confederation had chosen New York City as the place for launching the new government and had set the date for March 4, 1789. But the distances were great and the roads bad, and it was not until April 6 that both houses were able to raise a quorum. Only thirty-three days after his term had actually begun was George Washington officially proclaimed president of the United States.

The first president of the United States was John Adams, who had been elected vice-president but took the oath of office nine days before George Washington, Adams on April 21, 1789 and Washington on April 30.

After the Revolution, each of the states issued its own money.

The British Parliament, by a majority of one vote (178 to 177), passed a resolution recognizing the independence of the United States. The date was February 23, 1782.

Among the myths surrounding the young United States is that German almost became the official language but lost out to the English language by a single vote. In fact, the proposal before Philadelphia's 1796 Congress was not to adopt German but simply to provide for the publication of some laws in German translations so as to accommodate immigrants from that country.

Someone once bitterly remarked to Benjamin Franklin that the Constitution of the United States was a delu-

sion. "Where is all the happiness it is supposed to guarantee for us? Look at the bickering, the injustice, the
poverty," said the speaker. Franklin smiled at the man
and replied: "All the Constitution of the United States
guarantees, my friend, is the pursuit of happiness. You
have to catch up with it yourself."

Although George Washington's Farewell Address enjoined the young republic from entangling alliances, the
American people were mobilized for war with Napoleon
Bonaparte within two years of its delivery, and Washington himself was called from retirement to take command. And a brief sixteen years after the address the
American people were so deeply involved in European
wars that a foreign army (the British) not only invaded
the United States but burned the Capitol in Washington.

The first United States Congress, composed largely of
former revolutionary officers and signers of the Constitution, passed the Funding Bill, which enabled spec-
ulators—chiefly themselves—to make immense profits
by purchasing certificates issued to Revolutionary soldiers from them at current value, which was considerably below the face value, and then passing a law
whereby holders of the certificates were paid face value
by the government.

In the early days of the Republic, women were allowed to
vote. The State of New Jersey took away the feminine
ballot after an election scandal in 1806 in which, it was
said, every woman seemed to have voted "as many times
as she had dresses," while some men put on skirts to vote
a second time.

By 1774, Americans had achieved the highest standard of living of any nation in the world.

Voting wasn't always by secret ballot. In the 1800s it was done *viva voce* at the town hall, or indicated by raising one's hand at the public square. The ballot not being secret, the timorous voter tended to abstain rather than risk offending local magnates with his raised hand or spoken preference, or by walking up to the election judges to signify his choice.

There is no factual basis for the belief that George Washington wore wooden teeth. The choppers were fashioned from a pound of lead, and the reason he frowned was to hold his teeth in. If he had relaxed his face muscles, the heavily weighted false teeth would have dropped out of his mouth. President Washington found it awkward to pronounce the difficult *s* sounds with the ill-fitting dentures, which is why his Second Inaugural Address was only one page long. For a portrait sitting, artist Gilbert Stuart ordered construction of a special set of teeth carved from hippopotamus ivory for Washington in order to fill out his face. Artistically great, the plates were worthless for eating.

In 1781, an English clergyman called the idea that America would ever become a strong and unified empire "one of the idlest and most visionary notions ever conceived even by writers of romance." Predictions of the time emphasized that the United States would soon be begging King George III to take them back into the British Empire.

George III did not send a minister to the United States

until 1792 but he did receive John Adams as the newly liberated nation's first minister to England in 1785.

The young American republic was a nation in flux. Even before the War of 1812, nine of the original thirteen Colonies had already changed their capitals. New Hampshire's capital moved from Exeter to Concord, New York's from New York City to Albany, New Jersey's from Burlington and Perth Amboy to Trenton, Pennsylvania's from Philadelphia to Lancaster to Harrisburg, Delaware's from New Castle to Dover, Virginia's from Williamsburg to Richmond, North Carolina's from New Bern to Raleigh, South Carolina's from Charleston to Columbia, and Georgia's from Savannah to Augusta to Louisville to Milledgeville and eventually to Atlanta.

The life span of the American slave of the 1800s was hardly less than that of the whites, and approximately the same as that of the average citizen of France or Holland. And while American slaves normally lived to the age of thirty-six, a peasant in Ireland lived an average of only nineteen years. The slave owner safely guarded the lives of his slaves because they represented a substantial investment, and dangerous work was invariably allotted to white workers, particularly Irish immigrants.

After the Revolutionary War the Americans taxed themselves higher than the British had.

In George Washington's day, it was the custom at formal dinners and receptions in Virginia society for women to display ample cleavage, which was enhanced by the use of very tight stays. Some even rouged a nipple and exposed it, while others even more daring often plopped a rose petal or two between their breasts to be fingered by some gallant during the course of the evening's festivities. The more audacious gentleman would place the petal he had retrieved in his brandy snifter and drink it down while the lady from whom he had plucked it beamed at the attention showered upon her. Bobbing for rose petals constituted a major part of the enjoyment of the evening.

The circular design that thwarts the free and easy flow of traffic in Washington, D.C., was planned by French engineer Pierre Charles L'Enfant, after he had observed the mobs tear unhindered through the streets of Paris during the French Revolution.

The location of our nation's capital city on the banks of the Potomac between the old settlements of Alexandria in Virginia and Georgetown in Maryland was the result of a compromise between Virginian Thomas Jefferson and New Yorker Alexander Hamilton, in return for fiscal benefits Jefferson conceded to the northern states. George Washington himself selected the exact site and Paris-born Pierre L'Enfant laid out the city not only as the seat of government but also as a major port to rival Philadelphia and New York.

Lancaster, Pennsylvania, was the capital of the United States for one day. The memorable event occurred in September 1777, when British General Sir William Howe and his troops were approaching Philadelphia and the Congress and all government officials fled to Lancaster, sixty miles west of Philadelphia. On September 27, Congress met officially in session in the Lancaster County Courthouse, then located in the town square. However, the town was overcrowded and there was no room for the Congress, which accordingly decided after one day to move to York, twenty-five miles further west, and which remained there for nine months, from September 30, 1777 to June 27, 1778.

Although New York was the first capital of the new republic, Philadelphia was the second American capital and remained so from 1790 to 1800, when the seat of government moved to what was then known as Federal City.

The White House was at first not white, but was given that name by George Washington after his wife's plantation in Virginia. It was painted white for the first time in 1817 to cover up the damage done by the British, who burned it in the War of 1812.

The original White House architect was James Hoban. Hoban, an Irish-born architect, practiced in Charleston, South Carolina, and was the winner of the 1792 design competition for the proposed new executive mansion. One of those he triumphed over was Thomas Jefferson, who had submitted his entry anonymously. In the nineteenth century, the renowned architectural firm of McKim, Mead, and White renovated the historic building.

Benjamin Franklin was the fifteenth of seventeen children of Josiah Franklin, and the tenth and last of his father's sons. He acquired a reputation for sagacity and wit that made him immensely popular with the colonists. His *Poor Richard's Almanac*—the name being derived from Franklin's pen name of Richard Saunders—was filled with common-sense philosophy and clever sayings, many of which Franklin himself wrote. The most quoted axiom, popular to this day, is: "Early to bed, Early to rise, Makes a man Healthy, Wealthy and Wise."

The name *Poor Richard* could have well derived from Franklin's bank account rather than his almanac. The early records of the Bank of North America reveal that Franklin was overdrawn on at least three days of every week.

Franklin was the oldest signer of the Declaration of Independence and the Constitution of the United States. Born in Boston on January 17, 1706, he was the most versatile and talented man of his generation, having achieved worldwide recognition in nineteen different fields of endeavor, as a journalist, diplomat, essayist, publisher, printer, statesman, humanitarian, historian, scientist, philosopher, author, economist, educator, capitalist, linguist, mathematician, teacher, editor, and inventor. Yet with all his accomplishments, Benjamin Franklin attended school for only two years.

The oldest independent democracy in the Americas is Accompong, known as *Maroon Town*, an autonomous black commonwealth in the heart of the island of Jamaica, established nearly one hundred years before the Declaration of Independence.

The world's most literate and oldest functioning democracy might appear to be the United States or at least Great Britain. In fact it is neither, but is instead the small island republic of Iceland.

On July 3, 1826, Thomas Jefferson lay dying at his home in Monticello. "Is it the Fourth?" he asked. "It soon will be," his doctor said.

In Quincy, Massachusetts, lay John Adams, Jefferson's political opponent, ill beyond recovery. "Thomas Jefferson survives," were his last words.

There had been years of an intensely strained relationship between the two men. But while Adams's last words have been interpreted invidiously, they were in fact merely meant as a question, since the antagonists, like two boxers shaking hands after a bruising fight, had long since reconciled and had corresponded with mutual affection.

Alexander Hamilton became George Washington's chief of staff at the astonishing age of twenty.

As Washington's aide de camp during the Revolution, Hamilton became the son that the older man had never had, and Washington took the place of the father who had left young Alexander. Hamilton's later marriage into the powerful and wealthy Schuyler family provided him with a family of his own, and he took full advantage of his relationship with Washington and the Schuylers in his meteoric rise in government.

Alexander Hamilton and Thomas Jefferson were unrelenting foes, yet Hamilton's unstinting support of Jefferson won him the presidency in 1800. Hamilton threw his considerable weight behind Jefferson enabling the Virginian to beat out Aaron Burr in the runoff election. Alexander Hamilton and Aaron Burr were very much alike: both were ambitious and both were strong-willed. Both vied for political control of New York. Hamilton castigated Burr, saying Burr was "a dangerous man, and one who ought not be trusted with the reins of government." Burr's demand for a retraction led to the Burr–Hamilton duel on July 11, 1804 in Weehawken, New Jersey, in which Hamilton was mortally wounded. Hamilton's vituperative statement prompting the fatal affair of honor was not in derogation of Burr's run for the presidency in 1800. Significantly, Hamilton's utterance was made four years later and was calculated to keep Burr from the governorship of New York in 1804.

Two years before the duel, Hamilton's twenty-year-old son, Philip, had been carried into the house, dying, following a duel which was also fought in Weehawken, with an Aaron Burr adherent. Nonetheless, Alexander Hamilton, a married man with seven children to support, risked the same kind of death himself.

Something that is often found in history books is that the settlers from England lived in log cabins. In reality, they lived in English frame houses. The Swedes, settling in Delaware years later, built the first log cabins.

When George Washington ran for Virginia's House of Burgesses in 1757, the eager young campaigner wooed his 391 voters in a manner fit to stir the envy of a Tammany pol. Washington had his campaign manager serve up twenty-eight gallons of rum, fifty gallons of rum punch, thirty-four gallons of wine, forty-six gallons of beer, and two gallons of cider royal. The voters averaged a quart and a half and Washington was elected.

New England slave-ship captains would trade rum for a shipload of slaves, then sell the slaves in the West Indies for a cargo of blackstrap molasses, which they then carried to New England, where the molasses was traded for rum. With this new cargo they set sail for Africa and repeated the three-step process, making a tidy profit each time.

Gerrymandering, the rearrangement of political voting districts so as to favor the party in power, derives from Elbridge Gerry, early American statesman and governor of Massachusetts. The odd shape of one of the districts carved out by Gerry was described as resembling a salamander, which prompted a newsman to put the two words together and say that it resembled a gerrymander.

Colonists who decided to move west were called *pioneers* if they were among the first in the area; *settlers* if they tended to remain as farmers; *homesteaders* if they occupied land given free by the government to those who would develop it; and *squatters* if they settled on land owned by someone else. If they lived near the coast they were *coasters* and if near the border of a colony they were *borderers.*

Many unmarried women came in shiploads to the Colonies in the seventeenth and eighteenth centuries expecting to find a husband to pay their passage money. Women who did not find husbands as soon as they landed would often be sold as indentured servants.

The *Conestoga wagon* was built by Germans in the Pennsylvania Dutch country near Conestoga Creek for hauling farm products, but was destined to play a far greater role in the development of the young American republic. The wagon was a large and rugged vehicle twenty-five feet long and eleven feet high, weighed three thousand pounds, and was covered by canvas draped over arching hoops.

Beyond the purpose for which it was originally designed, the Conestoga was used by the British in 1755 to deliver military supplies in the French and Indian War. Its most important role, however, was to come in the westward migration of the colonists. Transporting settlers across the great plains toward the Pacific Ocean, the prairie schooners trekked west, forded rivers, protected the pioneers against the elements and, as legend has it, were pulled into circles to fight off marauding Indians. This function has been overglamorized, however, in that the true purpose of such encirclements was to keep the pioneers' horses, cows, sheep, hogs, and chickens from straying.

American Indians did not engage in battle during the winter months, and they did not post guards. This gave an enormous advantage to the white colonists. Another advantage was that Indians did not unite in battle, except

temporarily. Among the natives there were always indi-
viduals, even tribes, that fought on the side of the white
men, although the settlers seldom took the side of the
Indians.

5
Presidents I

GEORGE WASHINGTON WON the purse and person of Mrs. Martha Custis, and married her barely seven months after the death of her first husband. Martha was the prettiest as well as the richest widow in the colonies at the time of the marriage. To Washington's own estate of five thousand acres and forty-nine slaves she added substantially, providing seventeen thousand acres and three hundred slaves.

The father of his country sired no children of his own; his new wife Martha brought her daughter Patsy and son Jacky into the family. The teenage girl was sickly, and in 1773 Washington lost his "Dear Patsy Custis." Washington did not get along very well with his stepson. The young man was immature, always finding excuses for work not done and bills not paid. And he was a drop-out from King's College, known today as Columbia University.

George Washington was not born an American citizen and was not naturalized. He was born a British subject in the British colony of Virginia, which ultimately became part of the United States.

When Washington took command of the Continental Army in 1775, Dr. Rudolph Marx writes in *American*

Heritage magazine, the forty-three-year-old general was a man rendered hopelessly unfit for military duty by previous attacks of smallpox, influenza, tubercular pleurisy, typhoid, dysentery, and malaria. Yet, says Dr. Marx, despite his sickly condition, "we have no record that Washington was ever incapacitated during the Revolutionary War."

The General served throughout the entire eight-and-a-half years of the American Revolution without a single furlough, leave, or even a day's rest, and received no pay, but stated, "I will keep an exact account of my expenses and that is all I desire." His pay if he had accepted a salary would have totaled $449,261.51, which, converted into modern dollars, is somewhere between $4.5 and $22.5 million. He particularly itemized his expenses to the purveyors of spirits.

It was the first inaugural and nobody had remembered to inform Washington at what time the swearing-in would take place. A Senate committee was hastily formed and dispatched to escort the president-elect, after which followed an hour of watchful waiting. It was then discovered there was no Bible upon which to administer the oath, whereupon a messenger was hastily sent to a nearby Masonic lodge to borrow a copy of the Good Book.

George Washington had to borrow money so that he could journey to New York for his inauguration ceremonies. The Revolution had generated a false prosperity, and when it was over, the economy was disintegrating and money had become very tight. Everyone felt the pinch, even the first president-elect.

One of the most vital questions that confronted the first Congress was what title should be adopted in addressing the chief executive. It was felt that the title of "President" was too plebeian; many social clubs and industrial companies had presidents. A committee appointed for the purpose suggested "His Highness, the President of the United States of America, and Protector of their liberties." George Washington preferred the resounding title of "His High Mightiness," but this respectful designation, as well as "His Elective Majesty and His Excellency," were rejected. The question of what title to bestow never did get settled, and to this day the president of the United States may be addressed in whatever form seems appropriate for the occasion.

At his second inauguration, George Washington rode in an ornate carriage behind six silvery horses; he wore a black velvet suit, diamond shoe buckles, and long black stockings, and carried a cocked hat in one hand.

When Jefferson came to his inauguration he arrived alone, on horseback, tied the horse to a hitching post, and sauntered over to be sworn in.

The president of the United States complained bitterly that the press printed lies about his administration and attempted to ruin almost everything he was trying to do. He denounced the journalists' attacks, which he said were "outrages on common decency," and said that if "disregard for truth and fairness" and "wilfull and malignant misrepresentations continued," they might destroy the government. Which president made these scathing statements? Nixon? Jackson? Polk? None of them. The president was George Washington, whose badgering by the press has plagued every chief executive since then.

Among things named after George Washington are the nation's capital city, a state, a bridge, 7 mountains, 8 streams, 10 lakes, 33 counties, 9 colleges, 121 cities and villages, and 1 monument.

The famous painting entitled *Washington Crossing the Delaware* was executed in Dusseldorf, Germany, in 1851 by the German-American artist Emanuel Leutze. He used the Rhine for the Delaware and Germans for the American soldiers.

The painting is our best known and perhaps most admired historical painting. The original is huge—twelve feet five inches high and twenty-one feet four inches wide—and weighs eight hundred pounds. It depicts General George Washington and his desperate troops crossing the icy Delaware on Christmas night, 1776, one of the most dramatic events in America's history and a stratagem that enabled Washington's ragged, half-starved army to score an astonishing victory at a time when the war effort was on the brink of disaster.

The Spirit of '76 and Leutze's painting *Washington Crossing the Delaware* are anachronisms. In both paintings the Stars and Stripes is conspicuously displayed, although the flag had no existence before June 14, 1777, when it was officially adopted.

President Washington had an aversion to handshaking. In the belief that a handshake was beneath a president's dignity, he always stood by the fireplace and received visitors with a courtly bow. Even his best friends never rated a handshake.

There were scarcely 350 federal employees in Washington's administration—hardly more than the number of slaves and employees at Mount Vernon, and only four cabinet members: the secretary of state, secretary of the treasury, secretary of war, and postmaster general.

George Washington had no budget to supplement his annual income of twenty-five thousand dollars. The current White House has an operating budget of 1,695,000 dollars in addition to the president's salary, expense accounts, and other departmental budgets that add up to untold millions of dollars.

The story of the boy George Washington chopping down a cherry tree and confessing to his father, saying, "I cannot tell a lie" was itself a lie, and was fabricated by Mason Locke Weems, an ordained Anglican minister also known as Parson Weems. An enterprising bookseller, he enlivened his biography of Washington with platitudes and apocryphal bravado, which he wrote after Washington's demise.

The first president was not a good public speaker. He never even delivered his Farewell Address—he had it printed in a newspaper.

In Roman triumphal celebrations, a slave rode behind the victorious general, reminding him, "Caesar, thou art mortal!" For George Washington, such words of caution were not necessary. He accepted praise and honor for his military exploits, but in his role in civil government the father of our country was denounced by a large segment of the American population, and left the presidency exhausted and disillusioned.

"His century was over, and he with it," was the sad commentary when George Washington passed away in the last month of 1799. Coincidentally, Congressman Henry Lee of Virginia wrote the immortal words: "First in war, first in peace, first in the hearts of his countrymen." Washington was also known as "Father of His Country," a salutation bestowed on him by Henry Knox. He lived but two years after his second term had ended, and in his last moments of consciousness said, "I die hard."

Statesman, diplomat, philosopher, scientist, inventor, author, and architect, few men in history have had such awesome talents as Thomas Jefferson, who probably knew more than any other man of his generation. He became governor of Virginia, minister to France, secretary of state, vice-president, and then president of the United States.

He was in France when the Constitution was hammered out, and after its adoption, Jefferson insisted that the states ratify the first ten Amendments, known as the Bill of Rights, guaranteeing freedom of speech, press, and religion, trial by jury, and other safeguards of democracy. The Constitution itself contained no guarantee whatever of civil liberties.

[58]

In the presidential election of 1800, Aaron Burr had as many electoral college votes—seventy-three—as his rival Thomas Jefferson. But the House of Representatives, where each of the sixteen states would cast one vote and a clear majority of nine was needed to win, gave the nod to the Sage of Monticello. Burr was elected vice-president. On the first House ballot, neither had the necessary nine votes: Jefferson was backed by eight states and Burr by six, with two undecided. The two states with representatives deadlocked were Vermont and Maryland. Vermont's two representatives felt unrestrained animosity toward each other, while Maryland failed in a decisive vote for Burr through the courageous presence of a representative who was so near death's door that he had himself placed on a cot next to the voting chamber so that his vote could be recorded at each ballot. The crucial question throughout the stalemate was, "Is Joseph Nicholson still alive?"

The deadlock continued for seven days and thirty-five tense ballots with no decisive determination. Upon the start of the thirty-sixth ballot it was noted that one chair of the Vermont delegation was vacant—that of a Burr supporter who abstained from voting. Thus, the Virginian was named by ten states in the thirty-sixth and final ballot.

President James Madison's unique plan for national defense when hostilities with Great Britain seemed imminent was for the nation, instead of building its own fleet, to lease Portugal's navy.

Today, presidential candidates are seen and heard in millions of homes every day by way of radio and television, but it wasn't always so. In 1840 General William Henry Harrison defeated Martin Van Buren handily without saying anything at all and without even stirring from his home state of Ohio.

More recently, in 1978, gubernatorial candidate Allan Larsen of Idaho underscored his opponent's refusal to debate and arranged a televised confrontation with the camera focused on an empty chair. His performance helped one voter make up his mind: he cast a write-in vote for the empty chair.

The United States had three Presidents in one year. In 1841, Martin Van Buren's term expired on March 4; William Henry Harrison, the new president, passed away one month later and was succeeded by John C. Tyler.

The only president who never cast a vote was Zachary Taylor. He was too busy soldiering to vote. Taylor served in the War of 1812, the Indian Wars, and the Mexican War. He never stayed in one place long enough to qualify as a voter.

The first presidential interview with a newspaperwoman occurred in 1829. Anne Royall forced President John Quincy Adams to grant her an interview by sitting on his clothes while he bathed in the Potomac.

Andrew Jackson was the first president who did not come from a wealthy, well-established family.

Andrew Jackson weathered the first recorded assassination attempt on an American president in 1835 when
both of his assailant's pistols misfired. But Old Hickory
already had two pistol balls in him when he entered the
White House, the result of duels in his salad days. They
were removed more than twenty years later.

In February, 1825, Andrew Jackson led by a large margin
in both the popular and electoral votes, but with three
candidates opposing him, he failed to gain a majority.
The House, on its first and as it turned out only ballot,
gave the election to second-place John Quincy Adams,
some said because of a deal made with candidate Henry
Clay, who was rewarded with the appointment as secretary of state. To prevent a similar run-off in the electoral
college, the Twelfth Amendment to the Constitution,
which provides for separate balloting for president and
vice-president, was proposed and ratified.

Harvard University, in 1837, conferred an honorary degree upon Andrew Jackson, but ex-President John Quincy
Adams, aloof and arrogantly aristocratic (he had majored
in Greek classics and English literature at the school),
disdained the ceremony because he did not want to wit-
ness his alma mater's disgrace in honoring with her highest degree "a barbarian and savage who could scarcely
spell his own name." When the citation for his degree
was read in Latin, Old Hickory replied in kind, roaring,
"E pluribus unum, quid pro quo," according to biographer Marquis James.

Andrew Jackson was idolized by his followers, and at his
inauguration they poured into Washington in frenzied

adulation to share the triumph of their hero. They tramped into the White House in their muddy boots, crowded the streets, spat accurately, and swore glibly, these men in coonskin caps and buckskin jackets, yelling and shouting the praises of Old Hickory.

Once he made up his mind to accomplish a purpose, Andrew Jackson didn't worry too much about legality or method. Informed in 1830 by his attorney general that there was no law authorizing him to set up the national banking system, he ordered the nation's highest-ranking lawyer to "find a law that does or I will appoint an attorney general who will."

January 2 deserves to be declared a national holiday, because on that date in 1835 the United States of America had a balanced budget, the treasurer having on hand enough money to meet the nation's entire indebtedness upon the presentation of claims. Andrew Jackson was president and Levi Woodbury secretary of the treasury. Similar fortuitous conditions existed on the same date in 1836 and 1837.

Only after Andrew Jackson retired from the presidency did his followers completely forego the name Republicans and call themselves Democrats.

Martin Van Buren, in 1837, introduced the custom of having the old and new presidents ride together to the Capitol for the inauguration ceremony. On the way up, Jackson sat on the right, and on the return trip, Van

Buren sat on the right. This has been the custom ever since.

The United States had a president for one day. At twelve noon on March 4, 1849, Zachary Taylor was scheduled to succeed James Polk as president. But March 4 was a Sunday and Taylor, a religious mystic, refused to take the oath of office on the Sabbath. Thus, under the Succession Act, Senator David Rice Atchinson of Missouri, as president pro tempore of the Senate, automatically became president of the United States. He spent the day at the White House, met there with several senators, signed a number of commissions, and for the rest of the day entertained friends who called him "Mr. President," General Taylor taking over at noon on Monday, March 5.

Back in the days when passions over slavery fanned the political flames, new parties sprang up under such catchwords and banners as Barn-Burners, Free Soilers, and Know-Nothings. In the 1850s the American Party, better known as the Know-Nothings—an anti-immigrant party but directed particularly against the newly arrived Irish—achieved a brief success, electing six governors, dominating several state legislatures, and in 1856 even running their own candidate, former President Millard Fillmore, for president. Fillmore, however, lost out to James Buchanan.

Franklin Pierce, the fourteenth president, was the only president who served his full term [1853 to 1857] without making a single change in his cabinet.

Only once has an elected president been dumped and denied his party's nomination for a second term. Flabby James Buchanan, appointed in 1853 by Franklin Pierce as U.S. Ambassador to Great Britain, avoided the fierce domestic squabbles and passions over slavery and wrested the Democratic nomination from Pierce. One of the most decent persons ever to serve in elected office—not too well versed in foreign affairs but an expert in how to win friends and influence people—Pierce has the sad distinction of being the only man elected president of the United States to be refused a repeat term by his own party. Four other presidents who were denied renomination were John Tyler, Millard Fillmore, Andrew Johnson, and Chester Arthur, but all had originally been raised to power by the death of a president, and lacked the party loyalty that elected incumbents, such as Pierce, usually acquire.

This is a brief résumé of the career of Abraham Lincoln.

He failed in business in 1831.

He was defeated for the state legislature in 1832. Then he again failed in business in 1833.

He was elected to the state legislature in 1834. His sweetheart died in 1835, and he had a nervous breakdown in 1836.

He was defeated for Speaker in 1838. He was defeated for elector in 1840. He was defeated for Congress in 1843.

Finally, he was elected for one term in Congress in 1846 only to be defeated again for Congress in 1848.

He was defeated for the Senate in 1855 and was defeated for vice-president in 1856.

He was defeated again for the Senate in 1858.

Finally, in 1860 he was elected president of the United States.

Most people think that because Lincoln began his life in a log cabin, he was born in poverty. In fact, many families lived in log cabins during the early 1800s, and the Lincolns were as comfortable as their neighbors, with their two youngsters, Abraham and Sarah, being well fed and well clothed for the era.

We all know how young Abe Lincoln learned to read, lying on the bare floor, a candle at his elbow, puzzling out the words in an old Bible. And we know of his reputation as a rail splitter born in a log cabin. But Lincoln the budding lawyer had a thriving practice in Springfield, Illinois, where he pioneered as a corporation lawyer for the new railroads and canal companies, making fees of up to five thousand dollars, and where, with large investments in finance and real estate he was soon considered a very wealthy man.

Lincoln's presidential campaign of 1860 was not based on the abolition of slavery. He was elected on a platform promising free land and a railroad to the Pacific.

Abraham Lincoln was not elected by a majority vote in 1860. Fewer than 2 million of the 4.5 million persons casting ballots voted for him, and he did not carry a single southern state.

By the time Lincoln was sworn in as president, seven states had already seceded from the Union. Those who see Lincoln as a racist point to the fact that he did not fight the Civil War to free the slaves but to preserve the Union. In an 1862 letter to Horace Greeley, he stated: "If I could save the Union without freeing any slave I would do it."

Framed and hung on the wall of Lincoln's office were five sentences he had written. They tell a lot about the man. Here they are:

> If I tried to read, much less answer, all the attacks made on me, this shop might as well be closed for any other business.
> I do the very best I know how—the very best I can. I mean to keep doing so down to the very end.
> If the end brings me out all right, what is said against me won't amount to anything. If the end brings me out wrong, then ten angels swearing I was right would make no difference.

"God bless the Russians," jotted Lincoln's Secretary of the Navy in his diary when the Russian fleet dropped in at New York in 1863. His comment reflected the attitude of many toward this gesture of friendship, which cheered the North during a dark moment of the Civil War.

The Emancipation Proclamation did not free any slaves, as it applied only to slaves in states that were still in rebellion against the Union, and not to those in the slave-holding states that had chosen to stay with the Union. Since it applied to the enemy, it had no force of law, and as it was ignored by the Confederacy, no slave was set free.

1861. The nation was trembling on the verge of civil war, southern states were seceding, and president-elect Abraham Lincoln was in danger. To thwart a murder plot against him, he was spirited on a stretcher at Harrisburg, Pennsylvania, aboard a night train to Washington that was guarded by friends and private detectives, and arrived in the capital unheralded at six o'clock in the morning. On his inauguration day, extraordinary precautions were taken. In order to protect the presidential carriage from a surprise attack, the army's chief of staff, General Winfield Scott, put riflemen on the roofs of buildings along Pennsylvania Avenue, while soldiers from the regular army lined the route of the procession.

The invitation to Abraham Lincoln to speak at the dedication of Soldiers Cemetery at Gettysburg was a courtesy extended to the president of the United States. Edward Everett, renowned orator and former secretary of state, was selected to deliver the principal address. At the ceremonies, Everett spoke for one hour and fifty-seven minutes. Lincoln's brief remarks took only a few minutes. Everett's speech began: "Overlooking these broad fields now reposing from the labors of the waning year, the mighty Alleghenies dimly towering before us, the graves of our brethren beneath our feet, it is with hesitation that I raise my poor voice to break the eloquent silence of God and nature." After a smattering of applause upon the conclusion of the oration, Lincoln stood up and put on his steel-rimmed glasses. He placed his stovepipe hat on a chair and fumbled in his pocket for a wrinkled piece of paper that began: "Four score and . . ." His voice was thin and high and in less than five minutes he was through. The crowd applauded politely.

Lincoln did not write the speech he delivered at Gettysburg on the back of an envelope on his way to that town. He wrote the speech that was to become known as the Gettysburg Address two weeks in advance, and he wrote and rewrote it several times, on White House stationery.

The opposition press panned Lincoln unmercifully for the Gettysburg Address, the *Chicago Times* referring to it as "silly, dishwashy utterances."

On the night of Good Friday, April 14, 1865, five days after Lee's surrender at Appomattox, President Lincoln and his wife, accompanied by two young people, Clara Harris and her fiancé, Major Henry Rathbone, went to Ford's Theatre to see the English actress Florence Trenchard in *Our American Cousin.* The president was seated in the decorated presidential box at the front of the theater, stage left, when he was mortally shot by John Wilkes Booth, an actor and fanatical supporter of the Confederacy. Lincoln died the next morning across the street in the red brick house at 516 10th Street. The shot was fired at a predetermined moment in the play, just after the backwoodsman comic Asa denounced the scheming mother with the words "You sockdologizing old mantrap."

After firing the fatal shot, Booth leaped down onto the

stage, but his foot got caught in the American flag that decorated the presidential box and he fell, breaking his leg. He escaped from the theater on a horse that had been left for him at the stage door, but was shot down by federal troops twelve days later in Garrett's barn in Virginia.

One of the most curious and persistent legends in American history is that it was not Booth but another who was killed; that Booth got away through an unwatched door after the barn was set in flames, and that he lived for many years afterward in Texas and elsewhere under the assumed names of Ney, St. Helen, and Ryan, and committed suicide by taking arsenic at Enid, Oklahoma, in 1903. However, forty pounds of affidavits testify that the man shot in Garrett's barn was the legitimate John Wilkes Booth.

The funeral of Abraham Lincoln was the most ornate in American history. Yet from 1865 to 1901 his body was moved seventeen times, once being hidden for a period of two years in the cellar of a monument in his former home of Springfield, Illinois.

Five hundred songs have been written for or about Abraham Lincoln. Four hundred twenty are campaign songs, presidential numbers, minstrel, and comedy compositions, while about eighty are funeral dirges and memorial hymns. The total constitutes the greatest number of songs ever written about one man.

The deed that inspired the saying "His name is mud" was the setting of John Wilkes Booth's broken leg by Doctor Samuel A. Mudd. The Confederate sympathizer was sentenced to life in prison for aiding the assassin after he had shot and killed Lincoln.

The word *hooker* comes from the camp followers who set up shop near the Civil War encampment of General Joseph Hooker in downtown Washington. The soldiers were camped on Pennsylvania Avenue between the White House and the Capitol. The women were nearby in an area of the city that was known as Hooker's Division and became the capital's red-light district.

Among the unusual restrictions imposed by slave-holding Southerners upon slaves was the use of certain words. In pre-Civil War days slaves were not allowed to use "white" words. A black girl would be whipped if she said her *mother* sent her on an errand. *Mother* was a "white" word and she had to use the "black" word *Mammy*.

Robert Todd Lincoln, the only son who survived the sixteenth president, was secretary of war in President James A. Garfield's cabinet and, ironically, witnessed the shooting of Garfield in 1881. Twenty years later, in 1901, Robert Lincoln was at the Pan American Exposition in Buffalo when Leon Czolgosz fired two fatal bullets into President William McKinley. After McKinley's death, Robert Lincoln never again accepted White House invitations.

Andrew Johnson of Tennessee succeeded to the presidency in 1865, and was one of the most unlikely men ever to inherit the job. His most vexing problem centered upon the social upheaval that had been engendered by the Civil War. Johnson, like Lincoln, was a man of humble origins with scant formal education, but unlike Lincoln he lacked tact, understanding, and a conciliatory spirit. The stage was being set for a dramatic contest in the Senate, and in 1868 Johnson was impeached over his soft policy toward the defeated southern states, charged with violating the Tenure of Office Act of 1867, a law that had been passed specifically to curb him. The Act took away from the chief executive the power to remove from office any official whose nomination had required confirmation by the Senate in the first place.

The impeachment proceedings were instituted and relentlessly pursued by Senator Benjamin Franklin Wade of Ohio, who wanted to be president with an intensity that has been likened to insanity. Wade was president pro tem of the Senate, and if Johnson had been removed, there being no vice president, Wade, who stood next in the line of succession, would have been president of the United States.

The Senate failed by one vote to muster the two-thirds majority required for the conviction of Andrew Johnson. At the trial, Senator Edmund G. Ross of Kansas had cast the vote that acquitted Johnson and enabled him to finish his term of office—an action that ruined Ross financially and socially and destroyed his political career.

Despite the lack of cohesion that prevailed during Andrew Johnson's administration, much important legislation was accomplished. One of the most noteworthy acts was the purchase of Alaska, effected for $7.2 million in 1867, under the negotiations of Secretary of State William H. Seward, who was greatly criticized for having bought icefields, polar bears, and seals.

"Seward's Folly" and "Seward's Icebox" were among the derisive terms that bedevilled Secretary Seward for having negotiated the purchase of Alaska. The Czarist government that sold it had made claim to it as *Alashka*, the Russian version of *Al-ay-ek-sa*, which was the Aleut name for "Great Country." The Russian claim was predicated upon the expeditions of Vitus Bering, a Danish explorer in the employ of the Russian Navy.

During the turbulent era of Reconstruction, when General Robert E. Lee was under indictment for treason and facing a possible trial and even hanging, he remained such an idol of much of the nation that in 1868 the *New York Herald* urged his nomination for president by the Democrats, to counter the Republican candidacy of General Ulysses S. Grant.

Ulysses S. Grant, Rutherford B. Hayes, and James A. Garfield—the eighteenth, nineteenth, and twentieth presidents—were all Republicans, all born in Ohio, and all generals in the Union Army. They were also the only three consecutive chief executives to wear beards.

Grant, a notorious practical joker, used to hand out trick cigars that would explode when lit.

Grant was a curious and puzzling man. A failure in everything he touched before the Civil War, in the war he suddenly became great. A former captain in the U.S. Army, the forty-year-old Grant had resigned under a cloud occasioned by a drinking problem, and seemed destined to spend the rest of his life in obscurity. Except for a stint in the Mexican War, his career had largely been one of scrounging and aimlessness. After his resignation he sold firewood on the streets of St. Louis in an effort to support his family, and on the eve of the Civil War was working in his father's harness shop. Four years later, U. S. Grant, military victor at Chattanooga and Vicksburg and easily the most popular figure in the North, was in Washington to receive formal promotion to the rank of lieutenant general. He was the idol of the military throughout the war, and as they dispersed to their homes, the men in the ranks carried and spread the fame of "Unconditional Surrender" Grant to every city, hamlet, and crossroads of the United States.

Joseph Jefferson, who starred in *Rip Van Winkle* for many years, was once approached in a hotel lobby by a short, round-shouldered man in a tarnished military uniform who asked whether he was an actor. Irked by the non-recognition, Jefferson departed in a huff. Later he asked a bellboy, "Who was the nincompoop who didn't recognize me?" He was informed, "That was General Grant."

Grant's inauguration ended in a free-for-all. The ball was held in the north wing of the Treasury building, and five times more tickets were sold than the number of people the structure would accommodate.

The original Oval Office desk was given by Queen Victoria to President Rutherford B. Hayes in 1878 and is still in the White House.

Chester A. Arthur, the twenty-first president of the United States, took over upon the assassination of President Garfield. A large man distinguished by his mutton-chop sideburns and drooping mustache, and fond of mink-lined overcoats, Arthur was one of the more corrupt New York politicians. Yet Arthur proved to be one of the most enlightened presidents this nation ever had. He prevented raids on the Treasury by vetoing bills that appropriated huge sums for small harbors, sponsored a fair revision of the tariff, cleaned up corruption in the federal government, and pushed through the first civil service act, which has been called "The Magna Carta of civil service reform."

The only president's child born in the White House was Grover Cleveland's daughter Esther, his second child, whose birthday was September 9, 1893.

Richard Falley Cleveland, father of Grover, was a Presbyterian minister. His task was to bring up and educate a family of nine children on an annual income of six hundred dollars.

Grover Cleveland is the only president in American history to serve two nonconsecutive terms (1885 and 1893).

A young lawyer at the time of the Civil War, Cleveland was attacked as a draft dodger in the 1884 presidential campaign because he had hired someone to fight in his place. However, the accusation backfired when it was revealed that his opponent, James G. Blaine, had also hired a substitute.

Besides having avoided the Civil War by paying for a substitute, Cleveland had other ghosts in his past. Doubling as a hangman while serving as sheriff of Erie County, New York, he had sprung the trap under two murderers.

During the Cleveland administration the government had a surplus of $140 million, and the president was faced with the predicament of what to do with the money.

6
Manifest
Destiny

MUCH OF AMERICA WAS ACQUIRED not by conquest but by purchase. We bought the Louisiana territory from Napoleon; paid 5 million dollars to Spain to clear a title to the Floridas; paid Mexico large sums for land we won by conquest and an additional $10 million for the Gadsen Purchase to clear a route from Texas to California; and acquired Alaska from Russia for $7.2 million. We also fought Spain to free Cuba; paid Spain $20 million for Puerto Rico, the Philippines, and Guam; and gave Colombia $25 million for the Canal Zone.

The territories that comprise our fifty states were at various times ruled by seven foreign countries, all or part of the areas of thirty states having once been under British control; twenty-five under French; nineteen under Spanish; eight under Mexican; four under Dutch; two under Swedish; and two under Russian.

Until 1867, when the United States bought it, Alaska was known as Russian America.

The largest real-estate transaction in history was the Louisiana Purchase of 1803, when our government bought from France what is now the middle third of the United States—a piece of land five times larger than France itself—at a price of only four cents an acre. Alaska was purchased from Russia for two cents an acre.

Not all colonials who went west did so to establish permanent homesites. Many went for other reasons: the prospector with his grubstake in search of gold or silver, hoping to strike it rich; the fur trader with wampum, trinkets, and blankets and other merchandise to exchange for pelts and furs; and the hunter to track down buffalo, deer, wild turkeys, and other game.

Five years after voting in 1884 to accept the gift of the Statue of Liberty that stands in New York Harbor welcoming European immigrants, Congress passed the Exclusion Act, all but shutting tight the ports of the Pacific to Chinese immigrants. And in 1898, when Hawaii was annexed by the United States, the Exclusion Act was extended to that territory.

Buffalo Bill, born William Frederick Cody in 1845, got his nickname when, as a twenty-two-year-old cavalry officer put in charge of provisioning railway workers, he killed 4,289 bison in eighteen months.

Buffalo Bill and other Indian fighters wore their hair long to show the red men they were unafraid. The Indians believed that a man with his hair clipped short was afraid of being scalped.

Although the name *Wells Fargo* conjures up the image of ponies galloping across the American Wild West, both of its founders—Henry Wells and William Fargo—were easterners who lived in New York, Wells having made only one trip west and Fargo none at all.

With all of its thrilling and romantic association with the Wild West, the Pony Express lasted only a year and a half. The transcontinental telegraph, completed in 1861, brought the Express to a halt, costing its investors two hundred thousand dollars.

The Louisiana territory had been French, then Spanish, and then French again. Early in Jefferson's first administration Spain closed the port of New Orleans and then, in 1800, secretly ceded the region to Napoleon. Jefferson, considering this a threat to the United States, hastily dispatched James Monroe to France with an offer to buy New Orleans and, if possible, West Florida. Monroe did not succeed in obtaining the latter, but he did obtain New Orleans and the entire Louisiana territory from the French for $15 million.

The island nation of Haiti was directly responsible for the Louisiana Purchase. When, in 1803, Jefferson sent James Monroe to assist Robert Livingston, the American minister, in negotiating to buy New Orleans from the French government, France was in desperate circumstances. War between France and England was imminent, and Napoleon had sent an army to reconquer Haiti in an effort to reestablish a colonial empire in the New World.

However, when the Haitians, under the brave leadership of black leader Toussaint L'Ouverture, destroyed Napoleon's army, he realized he would not be able to hold onto the Louisiana Territory in a war with England, and decided to sell it to the United States while he still could.

On January 24, 1848, James Marshall, erecting a sawmill for his employer, John Sutter, in Eldorado County, in the lower Sacramento Valley of California, saw "something shiny in the ditch." News of the discovery of gold in California was soon followed by a thorough trampling of the northern part of the state. With the smell of gold in the air, the stampede of prospectors and hard rock miners became an invasion. Five hundred sailors deserted San Francisco ships to join the rush, while day laborers, farmers, merchants, and college students all found one way or another to get to California to join the search.

In booming San Francisco, the population exploded from a mere thousand to more than twenty-five thousand by 1852 and 380,000 by 1860—the last figure including three thousand prostitutes who came from eastern cities, South America, China, and Europe. Men arrived penniless and walked away millionaires. But while lucky miners could pick up five hundred dollars a day washing dirt, the life of the prospector was hard and often brutal. Claim jumping brought on brawls, which were often settled on the spot by blade or bullet.

Moreover, food was costly and beds were scarce, with many miners sleeping in hotel lobbies and on saloon floors. Newspapers sold for a dollar each and playing cards for five dollars, while a dish of bacon and eggs usually went for ten dollars. By 1850, when California was formally accepted as the thirty-first state, San Francisco was a city fallen to tattoo parlors, honky-tonk bars, and burlesque houses where buxom strippers entertained prospectors who paid in gold dust.

President James K. Polk's efforts to purchase California and other lands from Mexico met with rejection, whereupon the president sought from Congress a declaration of war on his assertion that Mexican soldiers had crossed into American territory and spilled American blood. But a young congressman from Illinois demanded that Polk demonstrate the exact spot on American soil where the attack had taken place. The president never answered Congressman Abraham Lincoln.

Through military action, the United States acquired vast areas of Mexico, and by the Guadalupe Hidalgo treaty of February 2, 1848, gobbled up more land than in the gigantic Louisiana Purchase. The vast territory eventually gained included all of Texas, the states of Arizona, Colorado, Nevada, New Mexico, and Utah, and Polk's prize, California. When President Polk asked the Senate to approve the Mexican treaty that gave this land to the United States, a dozen senators voted against the treaty because they wanted to annex all of Mexico.

As any western history buff knows, Wild Bill Hickok was holding aces and eights when Jack McCall shot him in the back at the No. 10 Saloon in Deadwood, South Dakota. The famous poker hand—which gamblers today call "The Dead Man's hand"—consisted of the ace of clubs, ace of spades, eight of clubs, and eight of spades. Hickok's fifth card was the nine of diamonds.

From Cheyenne to Dodge City, hair-trigger tempers helped stake the claim that "God did not make all men equal, Colonel Colt did." A gunman without his equalizer was as helpless as a cowboy without his saddle.

When President Jefferson sent out the Lewis and Clark Expedition, their ultimate destination was so uncertain that Jefferson gave them papers soliciting the good offices of our counsel in Batavia [now Djakarta], in Java, and at the Cape of Good Hope.

A slender thirteen-year-old Indian girl, pregnant with the child of a middle-aged French Canadian guide named Charbonneau who had won her in a gambling game, led the Lewis and Clark Expedition over dangerous country to the Pacific. Sacajawea, born among the Shoshones, braved every peril of the hazardous journey, acted as an interpreter, and mollified hostile Indian tribes.

The battle of the Little Big Horn, where Lieutenant Colonel George Armstrong Custer and his entire force of 108 were slain by the Sioux Indians, lasted only twenty minutes.

The shoestring of the original thirteen United States on the Atlantic coast had by 1851 spread clear across the continent. So rapid was the growth of the nation that the topic of an 1828 Harvard College debate was: "Can one man be president of the United States when it is eventually settled from the Atlantic to the Pacific?"

The team that argued "No" won the debate.

7
The
Melting Pot

ONE OF EVERY SIX AMERICANS is either wholly or partly of German ancestry, and belongs to the second largest population group in the United States. The largest group comprises persons of English-Scottish-Welsh descent.

There are at least 106 ethnic groups in the United States, including such little known groups as the Manx, who are immigrants from the Isle of Man in the Irish Sea; the Wends, who migrated to Texas from what is now East Germany; 70,000 Albanians, who live mainly in New England and New York City; 2,700 Schwenkfelders, an obscure German religious order with two members in President Reagan's original cabinet; and 300,000 Cape Verdeans, nearly as many as in the Cape Verde Islands.

The Cape Verdeans, concentrated in New Bedford, Pawtucket, Providence, and Boston, are descendants of white Portuguese and black Africans, an ethnic tapestry woven with threads from the Chinese, East Indians, Jews, and Moors. They refer to their exodus from their island country off the west coast of Africa as the only large-scale "voluntary" or non-slave emigration from Africa.

American Jews, although numbering only 3 percent of the population, are the recipients of more than 25 percent of the Nobel prizes awarded to all Americans.

Italian Americans can better be understood with the knowledge that Italy as we know it today came into existence in 1861, when the city-states that constituted the Italian "boot" united under a single form of government. Immigrants who left the relatively new country left it as Milanese, Calabrians, or Sicilians, and became Italians only after their arrival in America.

The first big wave of Chinese immigrants were the workers imported by the Central Pacific Railroad in the 1850s to lay track to the Pacific. At the time, the Caucasian Americans already living in California were fearful of the racial change it might bring.

As recently as the late 1800s, Chinese in the United States had no rights, and there were few cases in which a white man was punished for abusing or even murdering a Chinese man or woman. One example of this cruel injustice occurred when a white man accused of killing a Chinese was brought before Judge Roy Bean's court in Texas, where the Judge, consulting his lawbook, decreed, "I can't find nothing where it says it is against the law to kill a Chinaman."

At least part of the reason for the large Irish population of Boston is that when the Irish were leaving their native land in great numbers to settle in the United States, the fare from Ireland to Boston was $6.50 less than that from Ireland to New York.

Chinese laborers who flocked to these shores in the 1800s to work on the railroads translated many American words into their own language with picturesque clarity: elevator became *rise-descend machine,* soda water was *angry water,* a razor was called a *scrape-face-knife,* the railroad locomotive was a *fire cart,* and a match was a *self-come light.*

First-generation arrivals to America from Japan are called *Issei,* second-generation Japanese-Americans are called *Nisei,* and third-generation Americans of Japanese descent are called *Sansei.*

The Jewish presence at West Point dates back to the first class in 1802 where one of the two graduates was Simon Levy. Today the U.S. Military Academy records list sixty-two Jews among the total enrollment. Their attendance has gone largely unrecognized. Even Jewish parents are not fully aware that there are Jewish students at the Academy. Forty-five cadets including five women attend services at West Point's Jewish chapel, but kosher food is not served at the Academy and the cadet who enjoys borscht and blintzes, kishka and kreplach and other dishes mother used to make has to get along without. A substantial number of Jews have risen to become high ranking *line* officers. The list includes seven army generals, four air force generals and two admirals.

8
States

OF THE FIFTY STATES, thirty-four have no law requiring their presidential electors to vote the way their state's voters did.

The only state named after an American is the state of Washington, which honors our first president. When the territory of Washington was ready for statehood in 1889, it was due to be called Columbia, after the overpowering river that courses through the northwest region, but the legislature, fearful that the forty-second state would be confused with the District of Columbia, gave it the same name as the territory.

At one time, Hawaii was an independent kingdom with its own monarch and a system of nobles and royal etiquette that would have been a credit to Versailles. Missionaries from the United States were active on the islands in the 1800s and the growth of vital sugar and pineapple industries increased U.S. involvement. In 1884, the United States leased the naval base at Pearl Harbor. Once the nose of the camel gets in the tent, the whole camel moves in. The naval base led to the annexation of the islands in 1898 and their establishment in

1900 as a U.S. territory. In 1959 the Aloha State became the fiftieth state.

The lopsided vote for Hawaiian statehood in 1959 was a contrived subterfuge. Hawaiian voters were asked whether they wanted statehood, yes or no. They were not given the opportunity to vote for independence.

Kalakaua, King of Hawaii from 1874 to 1891, was a hard-living, pleasure-loving ruler. In a poker game he played with sugar baron Claus Spreckles, Kalakaua held four kings and in his elation bet every chip he had. Spreckles had four aces and started to rake in the pot when Kalakaua placed his big paw on the money. "Whassamatta you?" he demanded, claiming that the cards in his hand and his royal presence constituted five kings and five kings beats four aces, thereby winning him the marbles.

Nobody is sure whether this happened or not, but even scoffers agree that if it did not occur, it should have.

When the United States took over the independent monarchy of Hawaii in 1898, the local population had already been decimated by previous contact with Americans and Europeans. Polynesians, having been isolated from the rest of the world, had never been exposed to contagions of the white man and had not developed effective immunities, with the consequence that from the time of Captain Cook's discovery of the islands in 1778 infectious diseases ravaged the natives, cutting their number in half. To further aggravate the harmful exposure to the white man, the New England missionaries who had come to do good did good for themselves, as the Hawaiians say, and in no time at all acquired title to valuable lands and established themselves as owners of the economic resources. The whites were soon followed by Asians who picked up whatever scraps remained of the unwary Polynesians and their proud civilization.

In all Hawaii there are no native animals that are dangerous and no native plants with thorns.

Alaska has four time zones, since it is at the top of the globe, where the longitudinal lines of the Earth squeeze together.

Alaska is 100 times the size of Hawaii. Nome lies west of Honolulu, and Attu, at the end of the 1,100-mile Aleutian Islands chain, is closer to Tokyo than to Juneau, the capital of Alaska.

When gold was discovered in Nome, Alaska, in 1899, the population of that town mushroomed from less than one hundred to twenty thousand, jamming Nome with people from all parts of the world. Saloons and gambling houses flourished, dance halls prospered beyond all other activities, and piled on the wharf were silks from the Orient, spices from the East, and wine from the Rhine.

Less than two-and-a-half miles separate Russia's Big Diomede Island from Alaska's Little Diomede in the Bering Strait. Between the two islands runs the International Date Line, so that Big Diomede is not only in another country, but in another day. On a clear day on Big Diomede, you can see yesterday by looking eastward.

The 115 Eskimos who live on Little Diomede are the only persons in the United States who are allowed to pay their taxes with carved ivory instead of money.

Alaska is so big that the twenty-one smallest states in the United States would fit into it. And it is so sparsely populated that if New York City had the same ratio of residents per square mile, only fourteen people would be living in Manhattan.

"Remember the Alamo." The Alamo in San Antonio, shrine of Texas's liberty, is where in 1836 Colonel William Travis, commanding 188 men, held off for thirteen days three thousand Mexican soldiers under the command of General Santa Ana.

However, while the heroic defense of the Alamo by the Texans may give the impression that the Americans won a resounding victory, the Mexican battalion finally captured the fort and massacred the entire garrison.

The first proposal to secede from the Union was hatched in New England in 1804, under the sponsorship of Senator Timothy Pickering of Massachusetts, preceding the secession of the southern states by more than half a century. The conspirators promised Vice President Aaron Burr the presidency if he would bring New York into the cabal, but the grandiose plan was nipped in the bud by Alexander Hamilton and other strong nationalists.

South Carolina was the first state to secede from the Union; the secession occurred on December 20, 1860. Wednesday, January 9, 1861 was the kind of winter day the Southland rarely sees. The sun shone and temperatures rose, but there was a humidity in the air that made tempers short. Confederate artillery fired on federal troops at Fort Sumter, South Carolina, and sparked the

Civil War. The state was readmitted to the Union in 1868.

When Brigham Young selected a desolate, arid valley as the land for his people, he did not profess divine guidance or superior judgment. The Mormon patriarch stopped there because his people were too tired to go farther. They were weak and weary, and he knew his followers would never make it to the next mountain range. This place was as good as any for a stopping place.

Brigham Young was forty-six years old in 1847 as he led 148 Latter Day Saints from Nebraska to Utah's Great Salt Lake Valley, where he established the home of the Mormon Church. There the leader of the flock ruled his followers for thirty more years and along the way married seventeen times and begat fifty-six children. Today, of some five million Saints, no fewer than five thousand are direct descendents of Brigham Young.

At the time the Mormons settled in Utah they did so to leave the United States; Utah was then part of Mexico.

The word *deseret*, commonly associated with Utah, does not mean desert but *honeybee*. It connotes the characteristic faith and industriousness of the Mormons.

Among the Mormons, Jews are known as Gentiles, and Indians are thought to be descendants of the ancient Israelites.

[99]

The name Utah comes from an Indian word meaning "high up." The lowest spot in the state is 2,100 feet above sea level.

Texas, alone among the states of the Union, can, if it so chooses, split up into five states, each with its own governor and two United States senators. These rights were accorded the Lone Star State when it entered the Union in 1845. The state was part of Mexico from 1821 to 1836, and after 9 years and 301 days as an independent republic entered the United States by treaty, largely on its own terms.

The haste with which Nevada was granted statehood in 1864 was due to President Lincoln's efforts. Residents of the Nevada Territory did not want statehood, which they assumed would bring higher taxes, but Lincoln needed the support of the new state, which would add two votes to pass the Thirteenth Amendment outlawing slavery, and three votes in the upcoming presidential election. Lincoln signed the bill making Nevada a state only one week before the election, and Nevadans christened their state the "Battle-Born State."

Maine is the only state in the United States with a one-syllable name.

The State of Michigan expanded from 58,000 to 97,960 square miles without adding an inch of territory simply by incorporating into its area 39,960 miles of the Great Lakes that lie within the state's borders.

In one year, more than twenty thousand laws are passed in this country, and yet it is said that ignorance of the law is no excuse for a violation.

A law in Kansas provides that "When two trains approach each other at a crossing they must both come to a full stop and neither shall start until the other is gone."

In Arizona a gun or other weapon that has been used to kill game unlawfully is confiscated by the state. But a weapon that has killed a person must be returned to the defendant if he or she is not convicted or to an heir if the defendant is convicted.

The official legal tender of New Hampshire was not changed from pounds and shillings to dollars and cents until 1950.

Vermont was an independent nation from 1777 to 1791, coining its own money, running its own postal service, and carrying on diplomatic relations with foreign governments. It then became the fourteenth state of the Union and was known as New Connecticut. It was also the first state to forbid slavery.

On September 11, 1941, three months before Pearl Harbor, the Vermont Legislature officially declared "a state of belligerency with Germany."

A fleet of Chinese war junks set out to attack California in 1875, when the Emperor of China was informed that many Chinese working in the United States were being mistreated. The colorful Chinese ships with brass cannons sailed into Monterey harbor, ready to blast the city to pieces if it put up a fight. The people of Monterey, far from resisting, were so enchanted with this surprise visit that they welcomed the invaders to their community and showered them with gifts. Overwhelmed with the hospitality, the Oriental warriors decided not to return home, and instead remained in Monterey, with some getting work on the railroads and others as fishermen.

Louisiana is the only state in the Union named after a European king. The name honors Louis XIV of France.

Idaho is the only state in the United States over which no foreign flag has ever flown.

Six different flags have flown over Texas: the Fleur-de-lis of France; the Lions and Castles of Spain; the Eagle and Snake of Mexico; the Lone Star of the Republic of Texas; the Stars and Bars of the Confederacy; and the Stars and Stripes of the United States.

When a state is added to the Union, its star is added to the flag on July 4 following the date of its admission.

Two widespread misconceptions about the American flag are that each star represents a particular state, and that the stars are arranged in the order in which states entered the Union. Actually the stars represent the states collectively, not individually.

North Dakota and South Dakota were admitted at the same time, and since President Benjamin Harrison covered the proclamations of admission while signing them, it is not known which is the thirty-ninth and which the fortieth state of the Union.

The official name of Rhode Island is The State of Rhode Island and Providence Plantations. Originally called *Roode Eylandt* by the Dutch navigator Adrian Block, the state's name was later anglicized. Smallest of the states, its capital, Providence, has the biggest state capitol building in the nation.

Rhode Island declared its independence from Great Britain two months before the twelve other colonies. It is so small that no one is ever more than an hour away from any point within the state. California could fit thirty Rhode Islands within its border. Yet despite its high population density, nearly two-thirds of Rhode Island is open space. It has the longest name of any state and the shortest motto: *Hope.*

Less snow falls on the North Pole than on parts of Virginia. And according to noted explorer Vilhjalmur Stefansson, the annual snowfall of Ellesmere Island, the most northerly island yet discovered, is less than that of California.

North Dakota, Montana, and Wyoming are three states in which it often gets colder than at the North Pole.

George Washington must be the most highly regarded personage in New Jersey. There are no fewer than fourteen municipalities in the Garden State that are named after the Father of Our Country, including just plain Washington, Washington Valley, Washington Crossing, and Washingtonville, as well as six Washington Townships in Bergen, Burlington, Gloucester, Mercer, Morris, and Warren Counties. An admirable display of patriotism, the array can be downright confusing when you have to send a letter. Be sure it bears the correct ZIP code.

The name *Massachusetts* is derived from Indian words meaning "near the great hill." The hills in the eastern area of the state, where the Pilgrims landed and got the name, are where Indian tribes customarily met for powwows. The name *Connecticut* comes from Indian words meaning "beside the long tidal river." The two states are the only ones among the thirteen original Colonies to bear Indian names.

There is good reason why the codfish is an emblem of Massachusetts, and why its effigy, which hangs in the Massachusetts Statehouse, has been revered for two hundred years. Codfish saved the early settlers from starvation and, preserved with salt, became their first source of revenue as an export.

New York is not usually thought of as a state of firsts, but by 1614, six years before the Pilgrims settled at Plymouth, Albany was already established as a trading center and had its own fort.

New York State still has some twenty-eight thousand Indians, almost half of whom live on federal reservations. Many Manhattanites are not aware that 250 Shinnecocks and 167 Poospatucks live on small reservations at the eastern tip of Long Island. The State also has seventy Indian treaties that it must meet, including one with the Onondagas which, in addition to a regular annuity of cash, requires 150 bushels of salt.

One of every ten persons in America is a Californian. The number of Californians exceeds the number of Swedes, Norwegians, Danes, and Finns in Europe; outnumbers Australians and New Zealanders combined; and is twice as great as the number of Hungarians or Greeks. Of the last four presidents, two have been Californians and another has adopted the state. Were it considered as a nation, California's gross national product would be seventh among the countries of the world.

If you come across towns with such preposterous names as Sten, Gupton, Mamers, Vass, Method, and Wagram, and rivers called the Pee Dee and the Haw, you will know that you are passing through North Carolina.

Whether diamonds are a girl's best friend or merely a form of commodity investment, Murfreesboro, Arkansas, is the only known site in North America at which diamonds have been found. For two dollars you can dig, rake, or scrape for diamonds until the sun goes down, and keep anything you find. Most of the stones that are found are small, industrial-grade diamonds, but larger jewel-quality stones have occasionally been discovered.

While still a territory in 1869, Wyoming made world history by granting women the right to vote. Admitted to the Union as the forty-fourth state in 1890, it persistently maintained an equality of the sexes, and in 1924 elected Nellie Taylor Rose as the nation's first woman governor.

Michigan is called the *Wolverine State*, but that ferocious creature has never lived there. One of the nation's busiest maritime states, it is seven hundred miles from the sea.

Michigan came close to not being a state. After the Revolutionary War, Congress was loath to administer the territory, and its British inhabitants sent representatives to the Canadian Parliament for thirteen years.

Although with only 9,300 square miles New Hampshire is the forty-fourth largest state, and with 735,000 residents ranks forty-first in population, the New Hampshire primaries are the earliest in the nation, which gives the state a political influence out of all proportion to its size and population. When in 1916 the New Hampshire state legislature voted to hold a presidential primary every four years, the town meeting day throughout the state was the second Tuesday in March, and if the primaries were held on the same day, the legislators reasoned, the town halls would have to be heated only once during that month. Thus the extraordinary importance of New Hampshire at the national level was due to the practical compulsion for each locality to save a few dollars in coal.

Georgians, to their dismay, are called *crackers,* a name foisted upon them when settlers in the state were joined by a miscellaneous group of adventurers that included mule-drivers, who were called "crackers" for the way in which they cracked their whips.

9
Presidents II

PRESIDENT THEODORE ROOSEVELT, always an avid physical-fitness buff, became dissatisfied with the corpulent tendency of desk-bound Army officers and, in 1909, issued a decree requiring every officer to demonstrate his soundness by hiking fifty miles in three days or riding a horse one hundred miles in the same period. To overcome objections to the order, the former Rough Rider, then a robust fifty years old, rode horseback with three friends from Washington, D.C. to Warrenton, Virginia and back, completing the hundred-mile round trip in one day.

The likeness of Theodore Roosevelt best remembered is the staid politician's pose: wearing a pince-nez, hands at his lapels. Still and all, TR was the most theatrical of our presidents, and at times almost absurdly so. His favorite attire in the 1880s, when he spent considerable time at a ranch in the Dakotas, was an ornate cowboy get-up. Later, as police commissioner of New York City, Roosevelt often donned a black cloak and wide-brimmed hat on his nighttime rounds.

Theodore Roosevelt had much the same attitude toward trusts as W. C. Fields had toward children and small animals. In the 1904 election, Roosevelt accepted large gifts from industrialists J. P. Morgan, E. H. Harriman, and Henry D. Frick, but TR's trust-busting activities led Frick to comment, "We bought the son of a bitch, but he didn't stay bought."

During his presidency, Roosevelt, on the basis of a report that soldiers had been responsible for a riot at Brownsville, Texas, ordered dishonorable discharges for an entire black regiment allegedly involved in the fracas. He later partially rescinded the order and reinstated many of the men.

Those who have seen the Charlie Chaplin movie *City Lights* will recall the millionaire who, when he is drunk, showers Charlie with expensive presents and takes him into his house, but sobers up the next day and throws him out into the street. That frame of mind suggests Theodore Roosevelt's attitude toward William Howard Taft, the man he personally chose to succeed him as president of the United States. When Roosevelt left office, it was with the conviction that Taft, as his personally chosen successor, would carry forward the policies of the Roosevelt administration. But in 1912, when the time came for Taft's renomination, Roosevelt opposed him and, failing in having him dumped, ran against him as the nominee of the Progressive Bull Moose Party. This cost Taft the election and shooed Woodrow Wilson into the presidency.

The final tabulation of the popular vote gave Wilson 6,286,020 votes, Roosevelt 4,126,020, Taft 3,483,922, and Eugene Debs 897,011. The Electoral College vote was Wilson 435, Roosevelt 88, and Taft 8.

William Howard Taft was the first president [1908–12] to own an automobile; it was a steam-propelled vehicle.

Wilson's 1916 campaign slogan "He kept us out of war" was coined by the keynote speaker at the Democratic convention of that year, former Governor Martin H. Glynn of New York, stressing an administration of peace. Reelected to the presidency in 1916 largely on this campaign slogan, Woodrow Wilson, one month after his inauguration, declared war on Germany and its allies. Posters proclaiming "He kept us out of war" were still on billboards at the time.

Woodrow Wilson played twelve holes of golf on the day he declared war against Germany. The president was such a golf nut he had some balls painted black so that he could play in the snow.

The first American president to visit a foreign country was Woodrow Wilson, who sailed for Brest, France, on December 4, 1918, to negotiate a peace treaty ending World War I.

The formal presidential press conference was initiated by Woodrow Wilson on March 15, 1913, and the conferences were then held regularly until the United States entered World War I.

One president of the United States was part black. Noted historian Rexford Tugwell records that the story concerning the ancestry of Warren Harding became public at the time of his engagement to Florence Kling, although it had long been circulating in Marion, Ohio, where Harding had lived since 1882. That at least one of Harding's ancestors was Negro and had come from the West Indies two generations earlier emerged again when Harding was a presidential candidate.

In Harding's bid for the presidency, Edward Doheny, oil baron who was later mixed up in the Teapot Dome scandal, paid for a national advertising campaign to counteract reports that the candidate was of mixed blood. The ads featured photos of Harding's parents, showing them to be unmistakably white.

When elected, President Harding had promised an Administration of the "most experienced minds" in the country. He appointed Pittsburgh millionaire Andrew Mellon, a titan in finance and politics, as secretary of the treasury—an excellent selection in those exuberant times. Mellon, who was described by a friend as "the greatest secretary of the treasury since Hamilton," retained his post under both Coolidge and Hoover, and only the Depression revealed that Gulf Oil, Alcoa, and other interests of the Mellon family had been particularly favored by the head of the Treasury Department.

Calvin Coolidge may have been looking for a third-term draft when he made the cryptic statement, "I do not choose to run for president in 1928," but if so, he outsmarted himself. Neither his friends nor the politicians were sure just what the words meant. Whether he conscientiously preferred retirement or whether he expected his party to vote him in by acclamation has remained a secret. Only Grant and Theodore Roosevelt, until FDR, tried for a third term, and both were beaten—Grant in the primary and Roosevelt in the election.

At a White House reception, the wife of a cabinet member bet Calvin Coolidge that she could get more than two words out of him. He replied, "You lose."

Coolidge's successor as governor of Massachusetts, Channing H. Cox, once asked him how he managed to leave his office every day at 5:00 P.M., when it took Cox until 8:00 P.M. to see the same number of people. "You talk back," explained Coolidge.

The Twenty-Second Amendment to the Constitution, adopted in 1951, does not outlaw a third consecutive presidential term. One who has acceded to the presidency and whose first term is less than two years can try for a second and a third term.

The day after newly elected President Herbert C. Hoover initiated recovery measures against the Depression and arranged for Federal Reserve loans to commercial banks, he lamented to former President Coolidge over the severe criticism heaped upon his programs. "You can't expect calves running in the fields the day after you put the bulls to the cows," commiserated Coolidge. "No, I don't," disconsolately replied the president, "but I would expect to see contented cows."

Richard Milhous Nixon is credited with a brilliant diplomatic breakthrough as the first occupant of the Oval Office to have visited mainland China. But Herbert Hoover had been there before; he and his wife Lou Henry had gone to China on their honeymoon, and before becoming president, Hoover had worked for several years as a mining engineer and consultant to the Chinese government.

Hoover was the first president born west of the Mississippi. He kept in shape with a 7:00 A.M. medicine-ball workout with friends and government officials, who became known as the "Medicine Ball Cabinet."

Although the first White House telephone—which had a simple "1" as its number—dates back to May 10, 1878, Herbert Hoover was the first president to have a telephone in his office. The telephone had been in existence for fifty-three years before one was installed on the president's desk in 1929. Prior to that, the telephone had been located in a booth outside the Executive Office.

Prohibition spawned Al Capone, the most notorious gangster of the era. Capone seemed to possess an uncanny immunity to the law. Ironically, what finally did him in was not his bootlegging and violence, the gambling empire he controlled, or any of his multifarious criminal activities, but an inadvertent upstaging of the president.

President Hoover, as per custom, attended the Opening Day baseball game in Washington, D.C. The Washington Senators were playing the Boston Red Sox. To every president since William Howard Taft, the opening of the major league baseball season has meant the chance to toss out the first ball and make a hit with the fans. From the moment President Hoover entered the ball park he was surrounded by a throng of reporters, photographers, and newsreel cameramen who swept along with him.

His ruddy face and neatly pressed blue suit were brilliant in the hot sun and added to the theatricality of the spectacle. Thirty-five thousand fans in the ball park kept their eyes glued to the president. Mr. Hoover looked out at the crowd and smiled benignly as he waved in all directions. With ball in hand, President Hoover slowly wound up for the throw. There was a gentle patter of hand clapping as the baseball was caught on the field by one of the Senator's players. Suddenly a swift, sharp, explosive roar rose in crescendo and all eyes left the Chief Executive while newsmen and photographers vanished.

Someone else had entered the ball park. Mr. Hoover could not believe that a movie star or even a boxing champion was so popular as to draw all eyes away from the president of the United States. He looked to see who had caused the commotion. It was Al Capone.

Word went out directly from the White House and Capone soon became a lifetime resident of Alcatraz, the new federal penitentiary on a rock in San Francisco Bay.

"Herbert Hoover is certainly a wonder, and I wish we could make him president. There couldn't be a better one." In 1919, these words were written by the man who twelve years later would be Hoover's chief antagonist—Franklin Delano Roosevelt.

Franklin D. Roosevelt, who went to Groton, was the first American president to have graduated from a preparatory school. John F. Kennedy, a Choate alumnus, was the second.

Theodore Roosevelt and Franklin Delano Roosevelt were fourth cousins once removed.

Both young Roosevelts were graduates of Harvard, both attended the Columbia University Law School, and both left after the first year in an era when a year at Columbia Law was considered a sufficient stepping-stone for a young man with political ambitions.

Both were elected to the legislature of New York State.

Both were at one time assistant secretaries of the navy in Washington.

Both were governors of New York.

Both ran for the vice-presidency—Theodore Roosevelt on the ticket with William McKinley, Franklin Roosevelt as the running mate of James M. Cox.

Franklin married Eleanor Roosevelt, the niece of Theodore Roosevelt and daughter of his brother Elliott, who besides becoming FDR's father-in-law was also his godfather. The bride was given away by her uncle, the president.

Theodore Roosevelt had five children by his second wife: four boys and one girl. Franklin Roosevelt was also the father of five children, also four boys and one girl.

Franklin Delano Roosevelt was elected thirty-second president of the United States in 1932, and was inaugurated exactly thirty-two years after Theodore Roosevelt took the oath of office as president.

Both FDR and his successor, Harry S. Truman, did not permit direct quotations. Newsmen were allowed only to paraphrase or comment upon alleged statements. This enabled the chief executive to refute any assertions that met with disfavor, on the ground of having been misquoted or quoted out of context.

The first of Franklin D. Roosevelt's four terms as president was not a full four-year term of office. In accordance with the Twentieth Amendment, the inauguration of the President in 1936 took place on January 20, shortening the time since Roosevelt's first taking of office on March 4, 1932, to less than four years.

Franklin Delano Roosevelt was not loved by everyone, and indeed it was known that he was a man you either loved or hated, but one whom you never disregarded. The anti-Roosevelt crusade in the 1936 campaign included a satirical piece that embodied a picture of FDR depicted as Mother Goosevelt . . .

> Who lived in a shoe,
> She had a lot of children, but she knew what to do,
> She gave 'em a hand-out, they were all easy marks,
> A farm for to live on, some trees for their parks:
> A concreted highway, a maid and a car,
> A boondoggled bungalow equipped with a bar,
> And three meals a day of breakfast food oats,
> The smiling old lady was after their votes.

Sex and scandal are old partners in the federal government. Warren Gamaliel Harding carried on an affair with Nan Britton, sometimes in White House closets. After his demise, Nan accused Harding of having fathered her daughter and wrote a book that scandalized the presidency. Warren Harding's reputation as a lover was brought to the fore again when his biographer came across 250 letters written by the president to hometown paramour Mrs. Carrie Phillips, which Carrie prudently saved. Curiously, Carrie's husband, to complete the menage à trois, was a friend of the Harding family and the two couples often traveled together.

In 1892, Republicans were singing: "Ma, ma, where's my pa? He's in the White House, ha, ha, ha." The target was Grover Cleveland, who, when sheriff of Buffalo, during a moment of weakness enjoyed with several friends the favors of Maria Halpin, a free-and-easy widow with two grown children. The young widow gave birth to a son and because it was a team effort, it was not exactly clear who the father was, but Big Steve accepted responsibility and supported the infant.

During the Lincoln administration, Kate Chase Sprague, daughter of the Chief Justice and wife of a senator from Rhode Island, carried on openly with flamboyant, red-bearded Roscoe Conkling, Republican senator from New York.

Among the Founding Fathers, even George Washington—a man with an eye for a pretty face—was not immune from rumors during long absences from Martha. Fellow Virginian Thomas Jefferson was a representative of Congress in France and had a passionate love affair with Maria Cosway, an unhappily married and beautiful young Englishwoman. She left her husband in London and spent four months in Paris with her American lover. Jefferson then took as his mistress the handsome slave girl, Sally Hemings, half sister to his deceased wife.

Alexander Hamilton occasionally jumped the marital fence and strayed into fresh pastures. The American politician was surpassingly vain and egocentric and his encounters were well documented by Hamilton himself and included liaison with his wife's younger sister and entrapment by Maria Reynolds, wife of an unscrupulous speculator and con man. Hamilton was carrying on his affair with Mrs. Reynolds while paying blackmail to Maria's cognizant husband. Maria Reynolds was a completely promiscuous woman whose sexual appetite could only be satisfied by a number of men. Alexander's dalliance with Maria went on secretly once or twice a week for several months and ended only when James Reynolds, with a long background of questionable activities, was arrested for trying to fleece a former soldier.

Franklin and Eleanor Roosevelt suffered posthumous humiliation at the hands of their own children when Elliott wrote of his father's love affair with Lucy Rutherford, Eleanor's pretty social secretary; his parents' conjugal sex life (none after 1918); and Eleanor's infatuation with Lorena Hickock, stocky onetime AP reporter nine years her junior.

Hick was a more or less permanent guest of Eleanor's at the White House, and while Hick and Eleanor were cooing on the second floor, FDR's secretary, Missy LeHand, young, vivacious, and pretty, had taken residence at the White House on the third floor.

More recently, the name Judith Campbell became known for reported shenanigans with the White House occupant while she was involved in a similar relationship with two Mafia leaders.

On May 27, 1935, the U.S. Supreme Court unanimously decided that the National Industrial Recovery Act (NIRA) was null and void. Enthusiasm for the Act was already dying, and Roosevelt's New Deal, assailed by management and a number of labor leaders, was plagued by difficulties of enforcement. A demand for restoration of the free enterprise system was surging through the business community. Thus, the climate of opinion was prepared when Chief Justice Hughes, with the support of his colleagues, brushed aside the Recovery Act and threw its "Blue Eagle" emblem into the judicial waste basket.

Roosevelt was outraged at the decision. He denounced the conservative Justices' objections to New Deal programs as a relic of the "horse and buggy age."

In the 1936 election, the *Literary Digest* conducted a poll and sent out 10 million ballots. The poll showed that Alfred Landon would beat Franklin D. Roosevelt by a margin of four to three.

Politically liberal thinkers in the United States recognized that the New Deal of President Franklin Roosevelt was essentially the platform of the Socialist Party in 1904 and 1908. However, only a forceful and patrician individual such as FDR could have both sponsored these social and economic reforms and had them translated into law, and only in an emergency, such as the Depression. Lacking these factors, the American people would never have permitted the enactment of reforms so like those of the proletarian Socialist Party.

At the 1932 Democratic convention at Chicago, Roosevelt, who was the leading candidate, was dismissed by political commentator Walter Lippmann as "a pleasant man who, without any important qualifications for the office, would very much like to be president." Al Smith of New York, former Secretary of War Newton D. Baker of Ohio, Governor Albert Ritchie of Maryland, and John Nance Garner of Texas all had far more convincing credentials. Yet Roosevelt won the nomination on the fourth ballot, when a deal was struck with William Randolph Hearst, Garner's chief backer.

The rift between Al Smith and Roosevelt did not occur in 1932, when the latter won the presidential nomination even though Smith felt the party owed it to him. The break came four years earlier, when Smith had been nominated the Democratic presidential candidate. Identified as a Tammany Hall Catholic, Smith, who was governor of New York, had wanted as a successor a Protestant who had never been associated with the New York City political machine, and did everything he could to persuade Roosevelt to run for governor. Roosevelt, supporting Smith's candidacy, proved his loyalty to the hilt by consenting to run, and carried the state despite the Republican landslide. At the inauguration, Smith told FDR not to worry, that he was leaving an excellent staff behind. What caused the rupture between Roosevelt and the man he named "the Happy Warrior" took place the next day, when the new governor fired his predecessor's entire staff.

On December 8, 1941, President Roosevelt appeared before a joint session of the Senate and House of Representatives, and in a six-minute speech stated that December 7 was "a date which will live in infamy." The president asked Congress to declare a state of war against Japan. With an alacrity suggesting spontaneous combustion, the declaration was affirmed by both Houses, with one dis-

senting vote, that of Montana Congresswoman Jeannette
Rankin.

DEWEY BEATS TRUMAN, read the *Chicago Tribune*'s headline in expectation of a GOP landslide in 1948. All the
wiseacres and poll takers were saying Truman would be
humiliated by Thomas E. Dewey, the cocky Republican
with the toothbrush mustache. The rest, as they say, is
history, including the banner newspaper headline er-
roneously declaring Dewey the winner and a number of
publications that had gone to press before the final count
was in, with articles mistakenly written as though
Dewey had won.

When Harry Truman upset Dewey in 1948, Bob Hope
sent the president a one-word telegram: UNPACK. Truman treasured it.

Thomas E. Dewey first attracted national attention in
1935, when he prosecuted mobsters Lucky Luciano,
Dutch Schultz, and Louis "Lepke" Buchalter, all of
whom controlled gambling, loansharking, and prostitu-
tion rackets in New York. Then, elected district attorney, he brought down corrupt Tammany leader Jimmy
Hines in a trial that "completed Dewey's metamorphosis
from local figure to national hero." Running against Roosevelt in 1944 as the Republican standard bearer, he met
defeat at the hands of the wartime President. Four years
later, Dewey again was anointed the Republican standard bearer. Yet despite his conspicuous achievements,
Thomas E. Dewey is best remembered for his unexpected
defeat by Harry Truman in the 1948 presidential elec-

tion. Ironically, Dewey's conspicuous achievements were the cause of his defeats. The public does not want a prosecutor in the White House.

Harry Truman had one of the most interesting language patterns of any occupant of the White House. A cabinet member's wife, having heard the president refer to a politician's statement as "a lot of horse manure," suggested to the First Lady that she attempt to have the president moderate his language. Mrs. T answered, "You have no idea how long it has taken me to tone it down to that."

Toward the end of the Truman Administration, the president sponsored legislation that converted many appointive offices into civil service posts, for which he was vigorously lauded. In fact, however, the purpose and effect of the law was to freeze the jobs of thousands of Truman appointees so that they could not be replaced by the incoming Eisenhower Administration.

When a statue of Harry S. Truman was put up in Athens, the president himself expressed doubts about the wisdom of erecting a monument of a living person. "You never know," he said, "when you have to turn around and tear it down."

The most recent American president to serve two full terms was Dwight D. Eisenhower. Since his departure from the White House, one president has been assassinated in his first term, one has retired in some disgrace, one has resigned in utter disgrace, and two have been defeated at the polls. In contrast to this turbulence, the Eisenhower Administration seems in retrospect like a peaceful oasis.

The 1960 presidential election was decided by 118,574 votes. Since there were 166,256 precincts, a minimal change of one vote per precinct would have made the losing candidate president. The 1962 gubernatorial election in the state of Minnesota was even closer. The governor lost his bid for reelection by ninety-one votes among a total of 1,250,000 cast, or less than one vote per county.

John F. Kennedy, as a presidential aspirant in 1958, scored an instantaneous hit in D.C. at a Gridiron Club dinner in 1958 by opening his address with the statement that, "I have just received this telegram from my very practical father," and pulling out what was purportedly a telegram saying: "Dear Jack, don't buy a single vote more than is necessary. I'll be damned if I'll pay for a landslide."

The vilification of John F. Kennedy reached the point of the Hate Roosevelt enthusiasm of the mid-1930s, and culminated in a mimeographed letter circulated in Washington that spewed out these words:

Five thousand years ago, Moses said to the children of Israel, "Pick up thy shovels, mount thy asses and camels, and I will lead you to the Promised Land." Nearly five thousand years later, Roosevelt said, "Lay down your shovels, sit on your asses and light up a Camel;

this is the Promised Land." Now Kennedy is stealing your shovels, kicking your asses, raising the price of Camels, and taking over the Land of Promises.

When Kennedy took office, he said that Americans should not ask what their country can do for them but what they can do for their country. These were the exact words used by Cicero in an address to the Roman Senate in 63 B.C.

Ninety-eight minutes after John F. Kennedy was pronounced dead, Lyndon B. Johnson was sworn in as the thirty-sixth president of the United States.

When Lyndon Johnson had to take the oath of office in Dallas upon the death of President Kennedy, no one knew where to find a copy of the presidential oath, or who had the power to administer it. A phone call had to be put through to the attorney general in Washington. The presidential oath or affirmation consists of thirty-five words and is spelled out in Article II, Section 2 of the Constitution. There is no restriction on who may administer the oath to the incoming president.

As president, Johnson encouraged a kind of intimacy between himself and his staff that extended to a swimming break in the middle of a meeting, where everyone followed him into the White House pool. Johnson would strip down and swim naked, and insist that the others skinny-dip as well. According to Doris Kearns, a former aide who wrote an intimate psychological portrait of Johnson, it was also not unusual for the chief of state, when he had to go to the bathroom, to move the discussion there, Johnson continuing the conference while occupying the commode. Johnson's inclination for talking to visitors while on the toilet, his often scatological language, and a penchant for exhibiting his sexual organs were a form of enmity toward persons of culture.

The relationship between American presidents and Canadian prime ministers is not always one of pomp and ceremony with smiles and professions of good will and embroidered with friendly talk about the thousands of miles of undefended border between the two neighboring nations. At Camp David in 1965, President Johnson vented his anger at Canada's prime minister, Lester Pearson, for an anti-Vietnam War speech by pushing him against a porch railing, grabbing Pearson by the shirt collar, lifting him up, and shouting, "You pissed on my rug."

On a presidential trip to Italy in December 1967, a meeting between Lyndon Johnson and Pope Paul VI was arranged. In the exchange of gifts, the pope gave Johnson a beautiful fourteenth-century oil painting, while Johnson gave the pope a large plastic bust of himself.

Harry Truman always considered his appointment of Tom Clark to the Supreme Court to be the worst bit of typecasting since Gary Cooper played an architect. The unpredictable decisions of the justices have often confounded the presidents who appointed those justices. Richard Nixon was devastated when his own appointee Warren Burger ruled that he had to surrender the White House tapes. Justice Burger, gutsy, practical, and quotable, likes to call 'em as he sees 'em. With his white hair and resonant but gentle voice, the chief justice looks and sounds like Lewis Stone playing the judge in the old Andy Hardy movies.

After Oliver Wendell Holmes ruled against Theodore Roosevelt in a major antitrust case, the president who had appointed Holmes fumed: "I could carve out of a banana a judge with more backbone than that." Dwight Eisenhower called his selection of Earl Warren "the worst damn fool mistake I ever made."

Before they were laughed into mothballs, the uniforms worn by White House guards in the Nixon administration consisted of gaudy white tunics with shiny black leather caps. The uniforms made the guards look like characters in a European operetta, and were withdrawn a week after their first appearance.

At one daily briefing following the Watergate break-in, Ron Ziegler, Richard Nixon's press chief, said, "I will not comment on a third-rate burglary attempt."

The huge, red, ornate White House desk, known as the Wilson desk, used by a number of presidents, was not named after Woodrow Wilson. It belonged to Henry Wilson, an obscure vice-president under Ulysses S. Grant.

Gerald Ford, who was the odds-on favorite to be Ronald Reagan's running mate in the 1980 election, was by-passed primarily because he had moved his residence to

California. Had the two men run on the same ticket, the Twelfth Amendment, which provides that when both candidates on a ticket are from the same state, that state's electoral votes cannot be counted in the election, would have cost the Republicans California's forty-five electoral votes.

There will be no black cats in the White House during the Reagan Administration. Nancy Reagan admits to such superstitions as "Never put a hat on the bed"; "If you forget something, do not go back in the house"; and "If you put something on wrong-side out, you leave it on that way." She comes from a theatrical family, and show people tend to be superstitious; instead of wishing them good luck, you tell them to break a leg.

Ronald Reagan's inaugural ball was the most expensive in American history, costing $8 million (although the money did not come out of federal funds). In 1853, Franklin Pierce's inaugural—which his wife did not attend—had cost only $322. It was also the saddest of all inaugurations; the Pierces' son died in a train wreck on his way to attend the ceremonies in Washington.

10
Cities

S T. AUGUSTINE, FLORIDA, is the oldest city in the United States. Founded in August 1565, it was the first city on the continent of North America to be settled by Europeans, although San Juan, Puerto Rico—which also flies the American flag— is older, having been founded in 1510.

Although both Tokyo and New York have disputed for years which is the largest city in the world, Shanghai is tops in municipal population, with 10 million people. Tokyo rates second with 8.6 million, while New York, with 7.5 million denizens, occupies eighth place, following Mexico City, Cairo, Moscow, Peking, and Seoul. Los Angeles, the nation's second largest city, ranks twentieth worldwide.

The orderliness with which Washington, D.C., was laid out often leads to puzzlement over why the Treasury Building interrupts Pennsylvania Avenue, necessitating a sharp detour in that otherwise straight thoroughfare. The answer is that Andrew Jackson, tired of bickering about the site of the proposed structure, one day stuck his cane into the ground at random and announced "Here's where we build it."

The City of St. Paul was originally known as Pig's Eye. By 1841, however, the population of Minnesota had grown from six thousand to an estimated one hundred fifty thousand, and the inhabitants voted to change the name of their principal city to St. Paul.

The name "Pig's Eye" had come from an early fur trader of the region named Pierre "Pig's Eye" Parrant because of the peculiar look of one of his eyes. Parrant established a grog shop in what is now downtown St. Paul, and his establishment became so well known that the area acquired his name. But when the region's first Catholic priest built the village's first church, he dedicated it to St. Paul, "the apostle of the nations," and asked that the settlement be known by the same name, which was how the name change came about.

The city of Texarkana is unique in that it is located on the border between two states and is named after three states. An imaginary line down the main street separates Texarkana, Arkansas and Texarkana, Texas. Each town has its own mayor, police force, and local ordinances. The post office sits astride State Line Avenue and the postmark is "Texarkana Ar-Tx." The -ana part of the name comes from Louisiana, thirty miles away.

On a per capita basis, the wealthiest locality in the United States has been claimed for Palm Beach, Florida; Scarsdale, New York; Beverly Hills, California; Clayton, Missouri; Wellesley Hills, Massachusetts; Sewickley, Pennsylvania; and Bloomfield Hills, Michigan. However, according to the U.S. Census Bureau—which seems to be in the know about such statistics—the award belongs to Shaker Heights, a well-heeled suburb of Cleveland.

Although mention of the name Brooklyn usually elicits guffaws, the borough boasts many noted Brooklynites: Bobby Fisher, John Steinbeck, Woody Allen, Lena Horne, Sandy Koufax, Walt Whitman, Barbra Streisand, Robert Merrill, Isaac Asimov, Jackie Gleason, and George Gershwin.

More Brooklynites participated in World War II than natives or residents of any other borough or city in the United States.

New York is the only city in the nation that has exactly the same name as the state it is in; other towns or cities bearing the name of their state also carry the word *City* in their name. Among these are Oklahoma City, Jersey City, Iowa City, Texas City, Nebraska City, Maryland City, and Oregon City. There are also some towns and cities that bear the names of other states, such as Virginia City, Nevada, and Kansas City, Missouri.

Corona, a small thriving city in California, is the only locality in the United States whose boundaries form a perfect circle. However, the city's slogan, which was originally, "Corona, the city in a circle where the people are on the square," was eventually discarded.

Azusa, California, got its name when pioneers—deciding that the vicinity had everything worthwhile in the United States from A to Z—added the letters "A" and "Z" to "U.S.A." and used the combination to name their town.

There is a town called Christmas, Florida, and a Santa Claus, Indiana.

Oshkosh, Wisconsin, is not the only Oshkosh on the map. There is an Oshkosh, Nebraska, the slogan of which is "Where there is always nothing doing."

Philadelphia, with a population of forty thousand, was the largest city in the Colonies and the second largest English-speaking city—after London—in the world.

El Pueblo de Nuestra Señora La Reine de Los Angeles de Porciuncula—The Town of Our Lady the Queen of the Angels of Porciuncula—is the original name of the modern City of Los Angeles.

Of the forty-four founders of Los Angeles, twenty-six were black, and they left their heirs enormous tracts of land.

Maria Rita Valdez, a granddaughter of one of the founding fathers of Los Angeles, was bequeathed Rancho Rodeo de Las Aguas, known today as Beverly Hills. Francisco Reyes owned the entire San Fernando valley. He sold his property in 1790 and became mayor of Los Angeles. Had he retained his land it would today be among the richest estates in the world.

Los Angeles, generally regarded as the largest city in area in the United States, is a dismal second to Jacksonville,

Florida. Jacksonville covers 825 miles, Los Angeles 465. However, there are 2,900 square miles in the City and Borough of Sitka in the State of Alaska.

The largest Mexican community after Mexico City itself is in Los Angeles.

11
The
Supreme Court

SLIGHT OF BUILD, with a lean face and vibrant, blue-gray eyes, John Jay, famed New York lawyer, was named by George Washington as first chief justice of the United States. Profoundly bored with his duties at the Supreme Court, Jay engaged in various extracurricular activities, notably as a candidate for governor of New York. He lost in 1793, but undaunted, staged a comeback in 1795, won, and resigned from the bench. Moreover, President Washington liked to keep a good man occupied, and sent the chief justice to England in 1794 to negotiate a treaty.

More than half the chief justices of the United States never attended law school. Until the early twentieth century, lawyers, rather than attending school, more often learned their profession by reading law in law offices.

The only man in American history who was both president and chief justice of the United States was William Howard Taft.

There is no chief justice of the U.S. Supreme Court. The presiding officer is the chief justice of the United States. Title 28 of the U.S. Code sets out this distinction.

Many men appointed to the Supreme Court have been denied confirmation by the Senate. John Rutledge, in 1795, was the first to be nominated chief justice but not approved, although he had already served on the Supreme Court in 1790 and 1791, resigning in the latter year.

The others rejected were Alexander Wolcott, in 1811; John Spencer, in 1844; George Washington Woodward, in 1846; Jeremiah Black, in 1861; Ebenezer Hoar, in 1870; Wheeler Packham, in 1894; John J. J. Parker, in 1930; and U.S. Circuit Judges Clement F. Haynsworth, Jr. of South Carolina and G. Harrold Carswell of Florida, who were nominated by President Richard M. Nixon.

John Marshall, secretary of state in the administration of John Adams, was offered the chief justiceship by his lame-duck boss. He accepted and was confirmed by the Senate.

But Adams had a problem. No one wanted to fill the post of secretary of state for the period of only six weeks that remained in Adams's administration. The president therefore asked Marshall to handle both jobs, and the polite Virginian was glad to accommodate. He served as secretary of state in the morning and chief justice in the afternoon, although he took only one salary.

American history records exactly eight federal judges who have been impeached by the House of Representatives; of these, only four were convicted by the Senate and removed from office—the last in 1936.

[142]

Of all past and present justices of the U.S. Supreme Court, five were of foreign parentage and birth, and one, David Brewer, was born to an American family living in Turkey. George Sutherland and James Iredell came from England; James Wilson from Scotland; William Patterson from Ireland; and Felix Frankfurter from Austria.

There is no constitutional requirement that there be nine justices of the Supreme Court. The number has frequently varied. Originally the Supreme Court had only a chief justice and four associate justices.

In 1937, FDR's efforts to increase the number of Supreme Court justices with men sympathetic to his New Deal made some people wonder if the F in his name stood for Frankenstein. The president was balked by Congress and was accused of attempting to "pack" the Court and pervert the Constitution.

Whereas Roosevelt sought to alter the Supreme Court's decisions by packing it, Lincoln flagrantly ignored its decisions, Jackson dared Chief Justice John Marshall to enforce them, and Jefferson's conflict with the Court was incessant.

The office of chief justice of the United States is not mentioned in the Constitution, nor are the powers of the Supreme Court more than generally defined.

For two-and-a-half years after it was established in February 1790, the Supreme Court of the United States did not have an opportunity to hear a single case. Almost two decades later, the court still had so little prestige that it once held its sessions in a tavern while a room was prepared for it in the basement of the Capitol.

At the private conferences of U.S. Supreme Court justices, the newest member traditionally votes first, so that he or she will not be inhibited by the more senior justices.

In no nation in the world is a court of justice held in such high esteem as the United States Supreme Court. The Supreme Court not only decides how the law of Congress or of a state is to be interpreted, but also whether a federal or state law is constitutional. And since the decisions of the Court are made by a majority vote, the opinion of a single justice may overrule legislation passed by Congress and approved by the president.

Roger Brooke Taney, chief justice of the United States from 1836 to 1864, administered the oath of office to more presidents than any other man, having sworn in Martin Van Buren, William Henry Harrison, John C. Tyler, James K. Polk, Zachary Taylor, Millard Fillmore, Franklin Pierce, James Buchanan, and Abraham Lincoln.

John Marshall, who laid the cornerstone of America's legal structure, had just two months' legal training in his life.

Marbury v. Madison, the most famous case ever decided by the Supreme Court, marks a milestone in American constitutional history. Its background is not without drama. On the eve of his retirement from the presidency, crusty John Adams, possibly as a gesture of defiance to his successful opponent, made a number of judicial appointments. Among them was that of William Marbury as justice of the peace of the District of Columbia. Jefferson responded to Adams's challenge and instructed his secretary of state, James Madison, not to deliver Marbury his commission, after which Marbury sued for a *writ of mandamus.*

On February 24, 1803, Chief Justice of the United States John Marshall, a resourceful foe of Jefferson, calculated both to avoid an open fight with Jefferson (who, by the way, was his cousin), and to assert for the first time a prerogative of the Supreme Court in reviewing the constitutionality of federal law. Marshall dismissed Marbury's suit on the ground that the Supreme Court had no jurisdiction in the case, and at the same time pointed out that Section 13 of the Judiciary Act of 1789, which empowered the Supreme Court to issue writs of mandamus, was contrary to the Constitution and thus invalid.

The implication of Marshall's decision was that the Constitution, as the supreme law of the land, is above the will of Congress. Having staked out this great claim, the Supreme Court let it rest for well over half a century, until the fateful Dred Scott case in 1857.

Thus Chief Justice Marshall set a precedent for the far-reaching principle of *judicial review*—the right of the Supreme Court to pass judgment on acts of Congress.

Religion has been an important consideration in many appointments to the Supreme Court. During the twentieth century, for example, there was perceived to be a *Catholic Seat* on the Court. It has never been questioned that Warren G. Harding chose Pierce Butler, a Minnesota lawyer, for the court partly because he was Roman Catholic. And when President Harry Truman appointed a Protestant, Tom C. Clark, to replace Justice Robert Murphy, a Roman Catholic, after Murphy died in 1949, it was viewed as a departure from tradition.

Similarly, it has been accepted for most of this century that the court should have at least one Jewish member. That custom started with the appointment of Justice Louis D. Brandeis in 1916 and continued with the selection of Justices Benjamin Cardozo, Felix Frankfurter, Arthur L. Goldberg, and Abe Fortas. After Fortas resigned in 1969 the tradition was quietly allowed to lapse.

Chief Justice Charles Evans Hughes flunked the bar examinations three times. Other prominent lawyers and judges have also tripped up once or twice.

The uproar over the internment of West Coast Japanese in World War II as a violation of liberty is only now—forty years later—reaching a crescendo. Yet the constitutionality of the measure was upheld by the wartime Supreme Court, which included Justices Harlan Fiske Stone, Felix Frankfurter, Hugo Black, and William O. Douglas, who were all liberals.

Justice William O. Douglas served on the U.S. Supreme Court for thirty-seven years, two years longer than any other justice in American history. Both Franklin D. Roosevelt in 1944 and Harry S. Truman in 1948 wanted Douglas to run with them as their vice-presidential candidate.

As a teenager, Douglas worked for a time as a *stool pigeon* when authorities of Yakima, Washington, decided to get rid of the prostitutes that infested the city. The young man's task was to stroll up and down South Front Street, the heart of the red-light district, on Saturday and Sunday evenings, identifying the ladies of the night and pointing them out to the authorities.

To adapt the stock brokerage firm's television commercial somewhat: when Justice William O. Douglas spoke, the other justices listened. Douglas at forty was the youngest member of the court; only one justice in history, Joseph Story of Massachusetts, was appointed at a more youthful age (thirty-two). Douglas's brilliance and incredible productivity were so highly respected by his colleagues that once when Justice Whittaker was unable to draft a majority opinion, Douglas finished his dissent and then wrote Whittaker's opinion for him.

Douglas's fourth marriage was to Cathleen Heffernan, a fresh-faced blond woman forty-five years his junior. She had worked as a waitress and afterward earned a law degree. The marriage was considered a scandal in Washington, and prompted the suggestion that Douglas be impeached. However, the suggestion wasn't seriously considered, since it was made by Senator Strom Thurmond of South Carolina, who was himself married to a woman forty-four years younger than he.

In 1962 the United States Supreme Court ruled by a six-to-one vote that prescribing voluntary prayers for the public schools in New York State violates the United States Constitution. Nevertheless, in the curious balance of powers upon which our Constitution is based, manifestation of belief in God is acknowledged in both houses of Congress, where each day's session is opened with prayer.

12
War

IF YOU LIKE TO THINK in terms of war, every war has produced a president: the American Revolution, George Washington; the War of 1812, Andrew Jackson; the Indian wars, William Henry Harrison; the Mexican War, Zachary Taylor; the Civil War, Ulysses S. Grant; the Spanish-American War, Theodore Roosevelt; World War I, Herbert C. Hoover; and World War II, Dwight D. Eisenhower.

No American president has ever lost an election during wartime.

The American government spends untold billions to defend the United States against a possible Russian strike. Yet Russia is the only major power with whom our nation has maintained uniformly peaceful relations since before the Constitution. We have been at war with every other major power:

England: American war for independence, and War of 1812

Germany and Italy: World Wars I and II

Japan: World War II

Spain: Spanish-American War

France: Adverse combatants in the French and Indian War, and the XYZ Affair, which disrupted relations between both nations and culminated in an undeclared naval war (1798–1800) that began with the capture of the schooner *Retaliation* by the French off Guadeloupe.

China: The Boxer Rebellion (1899–1900), in which the Chinese revolt was crushed by the combined force of British, French, Italian, German, Austrian, Russian, Japanese, and American troops. China was forced to pay a huge indemnity and the United States got its share.

George Washington's farewell address enjoined the young Republic from entangling alliances, yet the American people, only two years after delivery of the address, were arming themselves in preparation for war with Napoleon Bonaparte, and Washington himself was summoned from retirement to take command. Hardly more than fourteen years later, foreign troops had invaded American soil and the Capitol in Washington was burned.

The colonists griped at the taxes imposed on them, but the per capita tax on the British themselves was forty times greater than that levied on the Americans. Besides, the sugar and stamp taxes were considerably smaller than similar taxes the British had to bear. In fact, the colonies bore only one-third the cost of the French and Indian War. With the French defeated and the Indians subdued, England had done her duty and was no longer needed to defend her New World possessions.

In the War of 1812, New England states, especially Vermont and Massachusetts, refused to send troops or lend money to the government, and even considered secession.

It is commonly believed that were it not for the War of 1812, much of what is now Canada would be a part of the United States. However, the conflict brought the differences between the Americans and the Canadians into focus. Many in both nations were against the war altogether, and the Canadian Provinces participated to only a small extent, as did the New England states. The War of 1812 was also the last important war in which Indians played a major role. Chippewas, Sioux, Sauk, and Mohawk were among the tribes that swarmed to the British cause and to whom the British promised territory of their own.

Admiral George Cockburn, in command of a British fleet, captured the defenseless city of Washington in August 1814 and ordered all books, papers, and pictures to be piled in a heap in the center of the Capitol and burned.

On September 13, 1813, Commodore Oliver Hazard Perry defeated the British in the Battle of Lake Erie. His famous words, "We have met the enemy and they are ours," have come down through American history. Less well known, however, is that "ours" was two ships, two brigs, one schooner, and one sloop.

The Battle of New Orleans, in which Andrew Jackson won a notable victory when he defeated a superior British force, was fought on January 8, 1815, two weeks after the War of 1812 had ended. Owing to poor communications, neither side knew that the Treaty of Ghent was signed on December 24, 1814, officially ending the war.

The Patricio Battalion in the Mexican War consisted of American deserters. They were mostly Irish-Americans who joined the Mexican army because there were no Catholic chaplains in the American military, and priests traveling with the Mexicans won them over.

In the Civil War, officers of the Confederacy were often accompanied by Negro servants.

If you were drafted during the Civil War, you could send a substitute in your place. And if you had trouble finding one, you could buy your way out for three hundred dollars.

There never was a battle between the *Monitor* and the *Merrimac*. The ship that fought the *Monitor* was named the *Virginia*. The South had captured the *Merrimac* earlier, raised her from the harbor bottom to which she had sunk, and reconstructed her as the new iron-clad *Virginia*.

Not all draft dodgers in the Civil War stayed at home. Many emigrated to South America, and thousands fled to Canada or Europe. In fact, a ship full of the escapees was stopped at sea, and all of its male passengers were brought back to New York.

The Ninth Massachusetts Infantry carried the flag of Ireland all through the Civil War. The outfit was made up entirely of men of Irish birth or parentage.

In military terms, the Civil War was significant for the large number of men who bought their exemptions, evaded the draft, and deserted their regiments, and for the thousands who failed to report for service. In fact, desertions grew so widespread that whole companies decamped at the same time.

During the Civil War, Russia maintained a friendly attitude toward the Union and did its best to keep the European nations neutral. And in an extraordinary gesture of good will, Russia, with its fleet in New York, "loaned" Admiral Farragut five hundred men for the attack on Mobile in 1863.

A most dramatic episode in the Civil War occurred on May 15, 1864, when 247 teenage cadets from Virginia Military Institute joined the Confederate forces in the full fury of the war and helped turn back a Union Army threat in the Shenandoah Valley. The beardless youths marched from their classrooms eighty miles through rain and mud for four days to take part in the bloody battle. Ten of the youths were killed and forty-seven wounded in the day-long combat. The Confederate defenders were commanded by Major General John C. Breckenridge, who had been vice-president of the United States under James Buchanan.

On January 25, 1898, the United States battleship *Maine* appeared in Havana harbor and its officers went ashore to see a bullfight. Far from being a model of stability, the battleship seemed to be waiting for a match to be struck, and on February 15, just after the bugler sounded taps, the *Maine* blew up, killing 266 American officers and crewmen.

No one has ever discovered just what caused the disaster. Some blamed the Spanish and others said it was a self-inflicted wound. A United States court of inquiry was unable to obtain evidence fixing responsibility for the explosion. "Remember the Maine" became a popular cry, and led to the Spanish-American War, a ten-week conflict in which Cuba, Puerto Rico, and the Philippines were freed of Spanish domination.

One of the best known men in American history is hardly known at all. He is Andrew Summers Rowan, a U.S. Army officer during the Spanish-American War who carried the message to Garcia. Calixto Garcia was the insurgent general who was hiding somewhere in the interior of Cuba. The American government had something of vital importance to tell Garcia, so the army picked Lieutenant Rowan to bring the message to the rebel leader. Rowan had written a book about Cuba that was so good nobody realized he had never been there so he drew the risky job of delivering the report behind the Spanish lines.

A Message to Garcia is the inspirational account of the heroism of the young lieutenant. Written by Elbert Hubbard in 1899, it is the most widely published secular writing of record. The New York Central Railroad ordered a hundred thousand reprints and insurance companies stuffed *Message* in pay envelopes and premium notices, while millions of copies were dispensed by industrial concerns to their employees. To date 115,000,000 copies in twenty-five languages have been distributed. The gist of Elbert Hubbard's writing was that Rowan did not ask where Garcia was hiding, who Mr. Garcia was, or "Why me?" He plunged into the Cuban jungle and delivered the government's message. To this day, no one knows what the message was.

Rowan's heroism was finally rewarded by a grateful nation twenty-four years later.

A single event in Europe triggered World War I, with the eventual involvement of the United States and total American casualties of 320,000. On June 28, 1914—their wedding anniversary—Francis Ferdinand, archduke of Austria, and his wife were reviewing troops at Sarajevo, Serbia, when both were killed by Serbian assassins. The archduke had been heir to the throne of Austria-Hungary before renouncing all claim to the throne because of his morganatic marriage, but had retained the right to review troops. On July 5, Germany announced its support of Austria in punishing Serbia for the assassination, knowing full well that this meant war with Serbia's ally, Russia, thus setting off the chain reaction that led to World War I.

At the World War I peace conference, President Wilson asked French Premier Georges Clemenceau where future historians would place the blame for the war. "That I do not know," the French premier replied. "But this I am sure of—they will not say Belgium invaded Germany."

Although the armistice ending World War I was signed at 5:00 A.M. on November 11, 1918, hostilities did not cease until 11:00 A.M. the same day; thus, the shooting went on for six additional hours. Marshal Foch of France had been willing to comply with the request that hostilities cease on November 8, while the German representatives communicated with their government regarding the terms, but General John J. Pershing, commander of the American forces, objected. He opposed any armistice at all, and wanted to push his troops through to Berlin.

Precisely at 7:53 A.M. on Sunday, December 7, 1941, Commander Mitsuo Fuchida, flying high above the island of Oahu, announced into his microphone the infamous code words *"Tora Tora Tora"* [Tiger Tiger Tiger], signifying to the warlords of Japan that the surprise attack on Pearl Harbor had caught the American Pacific fleet completely by surprise.

The attack lasted only two hours, but by the time it was over, eight American battleships in the harbor were sunk or damaged; many of our cruisers and destroyers were hit; all six major airfields on the island were wrecked; nearly every American plane was destroyed, and more than 2,400 American lives were lost.

There were five critical opportunities the United States missed that might have avoided the disaster:

1. On the evening before the attack, the FBI monitored a significant telephone call with highly suspicious overtones from Tokyo to a Japanese in Honolulu, but was put off by the military.

2. Early in the morning of December 7, an American

mine sweeper sighted a periscope outside the mouth of Pearl Harbor, but disregarded and never reported it.

3. Later that morning the conning tower of an unidentified submarine was sighted and a depth bomb was dropped by an American destroyer, but the U.S. Navy headquarters downplayed it.

4. At 7:00 A.M. that same morning, two army privates at the radar station on the northern tip of Oahu, near Kahuku, picked up an enormous number of blips on their screen and telephoned the information center, where an inexperienced lieutenant goofed. The Japanese planes were by now already winging toward the islands.

5. In Washington, D.C., General George Marshall, who knew that something vital was about to happen, alerted the Army and Navy brass in Honolulu by sending an ordinary telegram via Western Union. The telegram was handed to a Japanese messenger who dawdled on his way to the American military headquarters at Fort Shafter on Oahu, and delivered it to Lt. General Walter C. Short, commander of U.S. Army Forces in Hawaii, in the smoke and wreckage seven hours after the attack began.

The United States lost more men at Pearl Harbor than it lost in naval action in the Spanish-American War and World War I combined.

No act of espionage or sabotage was attributed to a Japanese-American during World War II.

During World War II it became necessary to establish a military title higher than four-star general, or to adopt the rank that in other countries is called a field marshal.

But General George Marshall objected to the latter possibility, saying, "I'll be damned if I'll let anyone call me Marshal Marshall. Nope, we'll just have five-star generals."

In late 1941, Manuel Quezon, first president of the Philippines, wanted a ship to evacuate him from the island of Corregidor, but General Douglas MacArthur said it could not be done. On January 3, 1942, Quezon issued an executive order that 500,000 dollars be transferred from the Philippine treasury in New York to MacArthur's personal account. On the day after the General was notified that the funds had been transferred, Quezon was put aboard an American submarine and taken to safety. MacArthur himself left Corregidor soon afterward.

General George Patton, the colorful and sometimes outrageous World War II commander who became a military folk hero, had hard sledding. At twelve years of age he still could not read, and it took "Old Blood and Guts" five years to get through West Point, from which he was able to graduate only by painstakingly memorizing his textbooks word for word.

"Four–Four–Two," as the 442d was known, was the most decorated World War II combat unit in the U.S. Army. The regiment suffered nine thousand casualties in action against the Nazis, and the "go-for-broke" spirit of the men earned them fifty-two Distinguished Service Crosses and a Congressional Medal of Honor.

The longest war in American history was the Vietnam War, which lasted from April 1961 to May 1975. Yet war was never officially declared by the president, Congress, or the North Vietnamese government.

During the war, American bombers dropped more tons of explosives on Vietnam than they dropped on all fronts in World War II.

13
Presidents III

THE ONLY THREE presidential elections in American history in which more than 80 percent of the electorate voted produced Presidents William Henry Harrison, Zachary Taylor, and Franklin Pierce.

Abraham Lincoln and Jefferson Davis, president of the Confederacy, were both born in log cabins in Kentucky within one year and one hundred miles of one another. Lincoln was born near Hodgenville in Hardin County on February 12, 1809, and Davis near Fairview in Christian County on June 3, 1808.

Extraordinary similarities surround the lives and deaths of Abraham Lincoln and John F. Kennedy. Lincoln was elected President in 1860 and Kennedy was elected President in 1960. Lincoln was elected to Congress in 1846 and Kennedy in 1946. The names of both men contain seven letters. Both men were shot from behind and in the head, and both were killed on a Friday in the presence of their wives. Both presidents were concerned with civil rights.

The successors of both presidents were named John-

son, and the names of these successors—Andrew Johnson and Lyndon Johnson—both contain thirteen letters.
Andrew Johnson was born in 1808, Lyndon Johnson in
1908.

John Wilkes Booth, Lincoln's assassin, was born in
1839, Lee Harvey Oswald, Kennedy's assassin, in 1939.
Both assassins' names each contain fifteen letters. Both
assassins were slain before they could stand trial for their
crimes, and both were southerners who espoused un-
popular ideas. Booth shot Lincoln in a theatre and ran to a
warehouse. Oswald shot Kennedy from a warehouse and
ran to a theatre.

Lincoln was shot in Ford's Theatre and Kennedy in a
Ford motor car. Lincoln's secretary advised him not to go
to the theatre and Kennedy's secretary advised him not to
go to Dallas. Lincoln's secretary was named Kennedy,
and Kennedy's secretary was named Lincoln.

Claes's two sons started the lines that produced Theodore and Franklin Roosevelt. Franklin was descended
from Jacobus van Rosenvelt, or, as he called himself,
James, while both Theodore and Eleanor Roosevelt—
who was the daughter of TR's brother Elliott—came
from Johannes van Rosenvelt.

The closest presidential election in American history occurred in 1876, when Rutherford B. Hayes beat out Samuel Tilden by a one-vote margin—185 electoral votes to
184. Yet Tilden had two-hundred-fifty thousand more of
the popular vote.

The man whose vote selected President Hayes was
Joseph F. Bradley, a justice of the Supreme Court from

1813 to 1892. As one of the fifteen members of the special commission delegated to settle the Hayes-Tilden election in 1877, his vote—the last and decisive one—gave Hayes the presidency.

Republicans contested the returns of Florida, Louisiana, South Carolina, and Oregon, all of whom favored Tilden, but without these four states Tilden, with 184 electoral college votes, would be one short of the necessary majority.

The Constitution provides that "The President of the Senate shall, in the Presence of the Senate and the House of Representatives open all the Certificates and the Votes shall then be counted." But counted by whom? If by the Republican Senate, the Hayes electors would be sustained; if by the Democratic House, the Tilden electors would prevail.

Congress set up an Electoral Commission consisting of five members of the House, five of the Senate, and five justices of the Supreme Court. The House selected three Democrats and two Republicans, the Senate three Republicans and two Democrats. Four of the justices were designate: two Republicans and two Democrats. The fifth justice was to be selected by the other four justices with the tacit understanding that Justice David Davis, an independent, would be chosen; but he had been elected to the U.S. Senate, and so Davis was replaced by Justice Bradley of New Jersey, a Republican.

Bradley first favored Tilden, but the night before the Commission was to vote, he had a late visitor—his personal friend Senator Frederick T. Frelinghuysen came by for a chat. An influential Republican, the affluent senator from New Jersey was a college classmate of Bradley from Rutgers in 1836. The next day Bradley switched to the Hayes side. Thus, by a majority of one, the Electoral Commission awarded all 19 disputed votes to Rutherford B. Hayes.

The question has persisted: Just what did Bradley and Frelinghuysen say to each other in that late evening conversation? One can only speculate on the senator's power of persuasion.

Herbert Hoover, Franklin Roosevelt, and John Kennedy were millionaires when they entered office, and money was unimportant to them. Money was also unimportant to Harry Truman, who enjoyed Bess Truman's home cooking and found nothing uncomfortable after his return to Independence, Missouri, where he and his wife had a helper by day. Dwight D. Eisenhower, however, enjoyed money, and under a special ruling of the Internal Revenue Service the World War II hero was allowed to keep the royalties from his books not as income but as capital gains. On the other hand, Lyndon Johnson, who was dirt poor when he first went to Congress in the 1930s, amassed a fortune without ever leaving government office. He earned no larger salary than $22,500 a year until 1960, but died leaving an estate reported at more than $20 million and was lord of a manor of 3,700 acres.

It is commonly believed that the worst trouncing ever given to the loser in a presidential election occurred in 1936, when Franklin D. Roosevelt got 523 electoral votes to only 8 for Alf Landon. Yet in 1820, James Monroe beat John Quincy Adams by 231 votes to 1.

The greatest number of convention ballots ever required to nominate a presidential candidate were the 103 ballots needed to break a deadlock between Alfred E. Smith and

William Gibbs McAdoo at the Democratic convention in New York City in 1924. Yet despite this, the eventual nominee, John W. Davis, lost the election.

Norman Thomas ran six times for the presidency on the Socialist ticket, losing each time. Practically his entire platform has since been enacted.

William Jennings Bryan, the renowned attorney and orator, ran for the presidency three times on the Democratic ticket and lost each time.

In 1920, Eugene V. Debs ran for president of the United States while serving a prison term, and won over nine hundred thousand votes.

Few today are aware that Herbert Hoover was the father of the eight-hour day and the hot school lunch. As long ago as 1919 Hoover was championing the cause of the establishment of a minimum wage, equal wages for women, nationally guaranteed health care, and a social security system.

John F. Kennedy was not the youngest president in American history; Theodore Roosevelt, who assumed office upon the death of President William McKinley on September 14, 1901, was the youngest man ever to hold the office. Forty-two years old, he grew a mustache to look older. At forty-three, Kennedy was the youngest elected president.

Gerald Ford does not have the distinction of being the nation's first left-handed president. Harry S. Truman, the thirty-third president, and James A. Garfield, the twentieth, were also left-handed. Garfield could still turn perfect handsprings at the age of forty-nine, and did one an hour before he was assassinated.

On January 30, 1835, Richard Lawrence, a housepainter, fired a gun at Andrew Jackson during a funeral service in the Capitol rotunda. On October 14, 1912, John Schrank, a saloonkeeper, fired a shot at Theodore Roosevelt as he was about to deliver a campaign speech in Milwaukee. Both would-be assassins escaped a guilty verdict on pleas of insanity.

At the time John Wilkes Booth shot Abraham Lincoln, the president was unprotected. His bodyguard had stepped out for a drink. When Lee Harvey Oswald shot John F. Kennedy, the president was guarded by twenty-eight Secret Service agents, and six hundred police had been deployed to protect him. In the fatal shooting of William McKinley, assassin Leon Czolgosz had to go through two columns of soldiers and police to reach the president, who at the time was closely surrounded by four detectives, four soldiers, and three Secret Service agents.

Presidents Hoover, Eisenhower, Lyndon Johnson, and Nixon all ordered presidential yachts to be put out of service on the ground that they involved unneeded expenditures. But all four men found the temptation to cruise on the Potomac irresistible and ultimately put the yachts back in service. The most intense use of a presidential yacht occurred during the Watergate brouhaha, when Richard Nixon made fifty-three trips, in contrast to the eight to twelve trips a year he had made from 1968 to 1972.

The cornerstone for the White House was laid on October 12, 1792, the three hundredth anniversary of Christopher Columbus's discovery of the New World.

The only president who did not occupy the White House was George Washington, since the seat of the government at the time was in Philadelphia.

The White House has been completely reconstructed twice: once because of destruction in the War of 1812, and again during the Truman Administration because of decay. The original unfinished house that Adams moved into had only six habitable rooms. Additions have swelled it to 132 rooms and 20 baths. It now has five elevators, a barber shop, a dentist's office, and a bomb shelter.

Never formally called the White House until a century after its completion, the name of the presidential mansion did not become official until 1902, when Theodore Roosevelt put it on his personal stationery. The building became so associated with the name that it almost seems to be a living entity.

Supposedly, no president can be arrested while in office for any crime whatsoever. However, Franklin Pierce and Ulysses S. Grant were arrested during their terms in office.

President Pierce, in 1853, accidentally ran down an elderly lady in his carriage one night. A constable named

Stanley Edelin placed the president under arrest and then released him.

President Grant was arrested in 1870 while driving too fast in his buggy between Eleventh and Twelfth streets in Washington's northwest section. Upon recognizing the culprit, the police officer who had arrested him was profuse with apologies, but the president replied: "Do your duty, officer!", and insisted upon going to the police station on Massachusetts Avenue between Ninth and Tenth streets, where he paid a twenty-dollar deposit that was forfeited in court the next day.

Court records proved that Grant had been arrested twice before for the same offense—on April 11 and July 1, 1866, before he became president.

President William Howard Taft once got stuck in a White House bathtub, and it required four plumbers with special cutters to get him out.

Musical-comedy producer Earl Carroll is credited by some with having closed the door on William Howard Taft's chances of defeating Woodrow Wilson in the 1912 presidential election. Carroll wrote a campaign song which contained the lines: "Get on the raft with Taft, boys; Get in the winning boat." However, Taft weighed 385 pounds, and the prospect of climbing in a boat with a man of Taft's build dismayed many voters.

The presidency does not necessarily shorten one's life. John Adams lived to be 90; James Madison, 85; Thomas Jefferson, 83; John Quincy Adams, 80; Martin Van Buren, 79; Andrew Jackson, 78; Dwight Eisenhower, 79; and Herbert Hoover, 90.

The oldest elected presidents and their ages when inaugurated were Ronald Reagan, 69; William Henry Harrison, 68; James Buchanan, 65; Zachary Taylor, 64; Dwight Eisenhower, 62; Andrew Jackson, 61; and John Adams, 61.

Of the eight presidents of the United States who died in office, only two—William Henry Harrison and Zachary Taylor—passed away in the White House. Abraham Lincoln died in the Peterson House in Washington, D.C.; James A. Garfield in Elberon, New Jersey; William McKinley in Buffalo; and Warren Harding in San Francisco. FDR passed away in Warm Springs, Georgia; and John F. Kennedy died in Dallas.

After leaving the White House, John C. Tyler, who was fifty-four years old when he left, fathered seven children; John Quincy Adams returned to Congress; Andrew Johnson returned to the Senate; and Thomas Jefferson founded the University of Virginia.

Jefferson left the White House in 1809 with his possessions in three mule-drawn wagons, and repaired to Monticello and his "people"—Jefferson's preferred name for his two-hundred-odd slaves. The tall, spare ex-president, straight as a gun barrel, rode the circuit of his broad acres every day in his overalls, supervising the agriculture that provided his livelihood.

Ulysses S. Grant was broke and indeed penniless for a time after leaving the presidency, while William Howard Taft went farthest after his term of office. President Warren Harding appointed him chief justice of the United States, making him the only man ever to have served both as president and chief justice.

Following his presidency, Theodore Roosevelt went on a safari in Africa, made a grand tour of Europe, had another try for the high office on the Bull Moose ticket in 1912, explored the Brazilian jungle, and was preparing to run for president once again in 1920, but died in 1919.

Harry Truman returned to Independence, Missouri after his term in office. When a reporter asked him what he did on his first day back home, the ex-president replied, in a tone that struck a responsive chord in every husband's heart: "I took the suitcases up to the attic."

In a poll to determine the best presidents of the United States, conducted in 1948 by Harvard historian Arthur Schlesinger, Sr., seventy-five historians and political scientists designated five past chief executives great, in the following order: Lincoln, Washington, Franklin D. Roosevelt, Wilson, and Jefferson. After the top group came the near great: Jackson, Theodore Roosevelt, Polk, Truman, John Adams, and Cleveland. A similar poll in 1969 yielded identical results for the great presidents.

History has shown that almost every American president has had an embarrassing relative who always said or did the wrong thing at the wrong time. Lyndon Johnson's brother Sam Houston Johnson wandered in and out of his brother's career, drank too much, and was occasionally given to writing a bad check. Billy Carter's involvement with Libyan dictator Muammar el-Qadaffi's effort to cultivate influence for Libya in the United States did not help his brother Jimmy's good intentions. Nor did F. Donald Nixon, Richard Nixon's younger brother, whose business deals included a shadowy $205,000 loan from Howard Hughes and an attachment to fugitive financier Robert L. Vesco, enhance RMN's tarnished image.

Abigail Adams had a scapegrace brother, but even more heartbreaking to her and the president was their son Charles, who was dissolute and dishonest. He took $6,000 his father had given him to invest. Charles was an alcoholic and he passed on destitute of a home, living on charity.

Benjamin Franklin's loyalist son was under arrest in New Jersey. Nor was Thomas Jefferson entirely free from familial embarrassment. A beloved granddaughter was married to an alcoholic, and two nephews, Lilburne and Isham Lewis, committed a murder. Andrew Jackson's wife Rachel, although she died before her husband's inauguration, was widely satirized as a country clod who smoked a pipe, while several decades later, Mary Todd Lincoln went on a shopping spree that left her $27,000 in debt.

President William McKinley's brother Abner brought shame on the McKinley name with his telegraph stock manipulations and gave the president's foes a field day. The Roosevelt clan was also caught up in the younger brother syndrome. It embraced Elliott, Theodore's brother and the father of Eleanor, who died of alcoholism at the age of seventy-four.

One likely way to win a bet is to challenge someone to name the order of succession to the presidency. The answer is that after the vice-president, the next in line to take over the office is the House speaker, followed by the Senate president pro tem, the secretary of state, and then the other cabinet officers. As a practical matter, however, this succession will probably never be realized, for if the vice-president should succeed the president, as Gerald Ford did Richard Nixon, the next incumbent in line would be the newly appointed vice-president, ad infinitum.

Three of our first five presidents died on July 4. John Adams and Thomas Jefferson died on the same day in 1826, and James Monroe died on July 4, 1831. On the other hand, President Calvin Coolidge was born on July 4, 1872.

In order to remove the chief executive of the United States from office, it is not necessary to go so far as the Romans did when they stabbed Caesar, the English when they beheaded Charles I, the French when they guillotined Marie Antoinette, or the Russians when they assassinated their czar. The Constitution provides for the removal from office of the president, vice-president, and all civil officers of the United States upon impeachment and conviction of certain crimes.

Any Air Force plane on which the president is traveling automatically becomes *Air Force One.*

Only one man in history was the son of a U.S. president and the father of another. John Scott Harrison was the son of William Henry Harrison and the father of Benjamin Harrison.

Ulysses S. Grant was the first West Point graduate to hold the office of the presidency. The second and only other was Dwight D. Eisenhower.

Related to more presidents than any other known person, Spencer W. Kimball was kin to John Adams, John Quincy Adams, Franklin Pierce, Chester A. Arthur, Grover Cleveland, Herbert Hoover, Richard M. Nixon, and Gerald Ford. Kimball, who was President of the Mormon Church, could boast such a fruitful family because his grandfather, who belonged to the church in the early, polygamous era, had forty-five wives.

Eleven generals have become president—George Washington, Andrew Jackson, William Henry Harrison, Zachary Taylor, Ulysses S. Grant, James A. Garfield, Rutherford B. Hayes, Franklin Pierce, Andrew Johnson, Benjamin Harrison, and Dwight D. Eisenhower. Yet no admiral has ever been nominated or elected president.

The president of the United States is not elected by direct popular vote. When you go into the voting booth, you are marking your ballot for a list of persons to represent your state in the electoral college. There are as many of these *electors* as your state has congressmen and senators, which means that your state has the same number of votes for president as it has members of both houses of Congress.

The Electoral College—with its "unit rule," whereby a candidate who wins a plurality in a state gets all of that state's votes—makes possible the election of a president who receives fewer popular votes than his opponent. This has occurred three times, in the elections won by John Quincy Adams, Rutherford B. Hayes, and Benjamin Harrison; it also almost happened in 1968, when Richard Nixon was elected, and in 1976 when Jimmy Carter was the winner.

At presidential inaugurations, the vice-president takes the oath of office before the president-elect. The *New York Law Journal* concluded that since the outgoing president's term expires at 12:00 noon on January 20 and because the official oath is administered first to the vice-president, for the ensuing several minutes, the vice-president is potentially president of the United States until the oath is administered to the incoming president.

A presidential candidate can win the elections by carrying just eleven states: California, Illinois, Indiana, Massachusetts, Michigan, New Jersey, New York, Florida, Pennsylvania, Texas, and Ohio. He can thus win with a popular vote of less than 24 million, even though 60 million votes are cast for his opponent.

Presidents elected in a zero year die in office.
   William Henry Harrison   1840
   Abraham Lincoln   1860
   James A. Garfield   1880
   William McKinley   1900
   Warren Harding   1920

Franklin D. Roosevelt 1940
John F. Kennedy 1960

The only president not elected in a zero year who died in office was Zachary Taylor; he died in 1850.

Every assassinated president's surname has contained either seven or eight letters—Lincoln 7, Garfield 8, McKinley 8, and Kennedy 7. Adding William H. Harrison (8) and Harding (7) who died in office, we find that in the past century, the only presidents whose surnames have had seven or eight letters and who did not die in office were Calvin Coolidge and Lyndon Johnson. However, both took the presidency because the incumbent president died in office.

Only thirteen women have lived to see their sons become president of the United States. In addition to Lillian Carter, they were the mothers of George Washington, James Madison, James Monroe, John Quincy Adams, James Polk, Andrew Johnson, Ulysses S. Grant, James A. Garfield, William McKinley, Franklin D. Roosevelt, Harry Truman, and John F. Kennedy.

Four presidents did not use their legal name: Ulysses S. Grant's Christian name was Hiram. He took his brother's name when he entered West Point on the brother's credentials. Grover Cleveland's first name was Stephen, Calvin Coolidge was really John, and Woodrow Wilson dropped his first name of Thomas to take the maiden name of his mother.

President Ford was christened Leslie King, Jr., but took his stepfather's name when his mother married Gerald R. Ford.

Speaking of names, Americans have never elected a Smith, Jones, or Brown as president of the United States. However, Abigail Smith, who never held office herself, was the wife of the second and mother of the sixth presidents.

James Buchanan was the only bachelor president, while Grover Cleveland was the only president to be married in the White House, delighting the nation but raising some eyebrows by marrying his legal ward, twenty-one-year-old Frances Folsom, the daughter of his deceased law partner. The other presidents who married during their terms of office were John Tyler and Woodrow Wilson, both for the second time.

Fifty-four-year-old John C. Tyler married twenty-four-year-old Julia Gardiner in the Church of the Ascension in New York on June 26, 1844, and Woodrow Wilson married Edith Bolling Galt at her home in Washington, D.C. on December 18, 1915. John Quincy Adams was married in the White House but not during his presidency; his father, John Adams, was president at the time.

Four presidents were married to women older than themselves: Martha Custis was eight months older than George Washington; Abigail Powers was two years senior to Millard Fillmore; Florence Kling was five years older than Warren Harding; and Thelma [Pat] Ryan was eight months older than Richard Nixon.

Florence Kling's father, a banker, attempted to forbid her marriage to Harding, stating flatly that he would be a failure.

If you want to be president, see to it you are not born in June. No president ever has been. The best months have been March, October, and November, each of which has produced five presidents.

All five bearded American presidents were Republicans. The first, Lincoln, was clean-shaven when elected, but gave in to a young girl, Grace Bedell, who wrote that she would get her three brothers to vote for him if he grew a beard.

Union hawks denounced the Lincolns because their eldest son Robert had not enlisted in the army. Robert finally joined up—after his father had gotten General Grant to find him a safe post at headquarters.

Jacqueline Bouvier Kennedy Onassis is only the second presidential widow to remarry. Her second husband was Greek multimillionaire Aristotle Onassis. Frances Folsom Cleveland, the first presidential widow to remarry, survived the president by thirty-nine years. Five years after his death she became the wife of Thomas Preston, a Princeton University professor.

The most exuberant first lady was the second Mrs. John Tyler, the former Julia Gardiner. The president's wife received guests while seated on a dais wearing a crownlike headdress. She was attended by a dozen maidens-in-waiting, and she enjoyed being called "Mrs. Presidentress."

Mrs. Mary Todd Lincoln, dumpy, small, and often over-dressed, wore rings over her gloves and spent too much for clothes, including two thousand dollars for her second inaugural gown. The president's wife has been described as selfish, spoiled, arrogant, rude, and crude. Once, however, when she complained so much about grocery prices that the White House grocer quit, President Lincoln called him into the Executive Office, put an arm around him, and asked him, "Can't you stand for fifteen minutes what I have stood for fifteen years?"

Abraham Lincoln, asked once whether his wife's people spelled their name with two *d*'s because it was more aristocratic that way, answered, "Well, God spells His name with one *d*, and I guess what's good enough for God should be good enough for my wife's family."

As first lady, Mary Todd Lincoln was overcome with an unusual obsession: she would go to the stores in downtown Washington, D.C., and purchase countless numbers of white gloves. This foible is documented by hundreds of retail receipts.

The term "First Lady" was reportedly coined in 1877 to refer to Mrs. Rutherford Burchard (Lucy) Hayes at the inauguration of her husband, the nineteenth president. It meant that for the first time, the president's wife was endowed with a public identity distinct from that of her husband. Mrs. Hayes was also the first First Lady with a college degree, yet for her stand against liquor she was ridiculed as "Lemonade Lucy" by disapproving Washingtonians. At state dinners, said Secretary of State William Evarts, the water flowed like champagne.

The original intention of the Constitution was that rather than being lost to the nation, the candidate receiving the second highest number of votes for president would be vice-president. Had that provision prevailed at the time of the resignation of Richard Nixon, Hubert Humphrey would have succeeded him as president. During the first three presidential elections, however, John Adams, as runner-up in the first election, was George Washington's vice-president, and Thomas Jefferson served as vice-president under John Adams.

The only administration in American history in which the president and vice-president belonged to opposition parties was that of John Adams, a Federalist, whose vice-president, Thomas Jefferson, was a Democratic-Republican. Lincoln's vice-president, Andrew Johnson, was a Democrat; however, notwithstanding his party affiliation, Johnson was nominated by the Republicans and ran on the Republican ticket.

Gerald Ford was both vice-president and president without having been elected to either office.

Other than Spiro Agnew, the only vice-president to resign the office was John C. Calhoun, who did so voluntarily. Calhoun planned his resignation craftily; he remained in office until he became senator-elect from South Carolina, and was a lame duck vice-president when he resigned on December 28, 1832.

Aaron Burr, even after killing Alexander Hamilton in their famous duel, did not resign as vice-president. Burr slinked out of town and hid until his term had expired.

While the vice-presidency may appear to be a particularly advantageous springboard to the presidency, the American voting public has promoted only three vice-presidents directly to president: John Adams, Thomas Jefferson, and Martin Van Buren.

14
Americana

ALEXANDER HAMILTON'S real name was Levine. His mother, Rachel Levine, was married to John Michael Levine of the Danish island of St. Croix and did not divorce her husband until 1759. Alexander was born January 11, 1755. Later Mrs. Levine married James Hamilton, and Alexander took his stepfather's name.

"The Star-Spangled Banner" is the only national anthem that begins and ends with a question.

Figures released by the Federal Reserve suggest that if all the money in circulation were divided equally, every person in the United States would have $542.82. What the figures failed to add was that if the national debt were divided the same way, every person would owe approximately $3,473.00.

By the time you read this sentence the United States Government will have spent $235,000—but you have to read quickly.

After we paid Napoleon $15 million in 1803 for the huge areas embraced by the Louisiana Purchase, we paid Indian tribes more than twenty times that amount for the same territory.

On the other hand, the Indians who sold Manhattan Island to Peter Minuit in 1626 for $24 worth of trinkets got the best of the deal. Had they put the money into the Bank of England at 6 percent compound interest, they would have more than the entire net worth of Manhattan today. Besides, they did not even own the land. They were Canarsies, Montauks and Rockaways just in town for a visit. Minuit had to buy the land again from a tribe "uptown."

The United States of America is regarded as a democracy with a Chief Executive elected by a majority of the People. We have had forty Presidencies in which fifteen were minority Presidents, while nine Presidents were not even elected to the highest office, but succeeded to the Presidency when the President died or resigned. Moreover, eleven Presidents were army generals and achieved the Presidency not because they were especially fit for it, but because of their war exploits.

There are not fifty states in the United States. Our nation consists of forty-six states and four commonwealths, namely Virginia, Kentucky, Massachusetts, and Pennsylvania. How does a commonwealth differ from a state? "Commonwealth" originally connoted the idea of self-government more than "state" did.

The epitome of Lincoln worship is attributed to an unidentified freshman at the University of Wisconsin. Reported the student, "Abraham Lincoln was born in a log cabin which he built with his own hands."

Are you alarmed by the number thirteen? Our nation is loaded with thirteens. '76 adds up to 13. We started with 13 colonies and a 13 letter slogan: *E Pluribus Unum.* Our Great Seal has 13 stars, 13 stripes, 13 arrows, 13 leaves, and our eagle has 13 feathers in each wing. The flag has 13 stripes and began with 13 stars.

Jefferson was born on April 13, 1743. Washington was elected April 13, 1789 and Francis Scott Key wrote "The Star-Spangled Banner" on September 13, 1814.

Curiously, there are 13 letters in the name Richard M. Nixon.

In the aftermath of the Teapot Dome scandal of the Harding administration, Secretary of the Interior Albert B. Fall was convicted of the crime of having accepted a bribe from Edward L. Doheny, and Doheny was acquitted of having given Secretary Fall the bribe.

Warren G. Harding was imposed upon by corrupt acquaintances and died discredited. His father once said, "Warren, it's a lucky thing you were not born a girl because you can't say no." Harding often told the story himself.

Like Edsel and Waterloo, the Bay of Pigs has entered the vernacular as a euphemism for defeat. To everyone's surprise Cuba is not a small island: it is 800 miles long. A map of Cuba superimposed upon a map of the United States would extend from New York to Chicago.

Mother Goose was a Bostonian. In the 1600s the Goose family owned almost half of the city of Boston. Isaac Goose was the father of ten little Gooses, and he took for his second wife Elizabeth Foster, who had ten children of her own and thereby became the immortal Mother Goose.

Two presidents were known to have fathered illegitimate children. Grover Cleveland acknowledged his; Warren G. Harding remained silent.

However, Thomas Jefferson, a foe of slavery, had a mistress named Sally Heming, a slave of his own. She bore him four children, who were never acknowledged.

The Magna Carta, a key document in the evolution of personal liberties, was, strictly speaking, not signed by King John; he simply sealed it. In fact, there is serious doubt that he could even write.

Aaron Burr was convicted of adultery at the age of eighty.

Florida is west of the Panama Canal, but Miami is east of Havana.

To go from the Atlantic Ocean to the Pacific Ocean through the Panama Canal, you travel from west to east.

From Detroit to Canada, travel south. You'll wind up at Windsor, Ontario.

It is generally known that Reno is west of Los Angeles, but very few people know that the City of Valparaiso on the west coast of Chile is east of New York City.

Washington, D.C. is closer to Moscow in Russia than it

is to the capital of what state? Answer: Honolulu, Hawaii.

And what state is farthest east? Alaska, since it crosses the 189th meridian, where the East begins.

Charles Evans Hughes thought he had won the election when he went to bed election night. It looked like a sure bet that he would soon be sleeping in the White House. But the late returns from California changed his plans. When a reporter called to ask Hughes to comment on his defeat by Wilson, a valet said, "The President has retired." "When he wakes up," the reporter said, "tell him he's no longer President."

The original name of the Roosevelt family was Martensen. Claes Martensen, a sturdy Hollander, came to America in 1650 where he added "van Rosenvelt" to his name to indicate the town he had come from in the old country, and he became known as Claes van Rosenvelt, meaning "from the world of roses."

George Washington's birthday is actually February 11th, not the 22nd. The calendar was changed during his lifetime. In 1752 Great Britain and her colonies, including America, adopted the Gregorian calendar in place of the Julian, and eleven days were lost.

When the Gregorian calendar was adopted, making the year shorter by eleven days, irate Cockneys threatened a revolution to compel Parliament to "give us back our fortnight."

[191]

San Marcos University in Peru is older than Harvard. It was founded in 1551, eighty-five years before America's oldest university.

If anyone should ask you from where to where was Washington crossing the Delaware River, the answer is from Pennsylvania to New Jersey.

During an early debate on the expenditures for the Air Force, an economy-minded Congressman once exploded: "Why all this talk about airplanes—the Army already has one, hasn't it?"

January 1, 1900 was not the first day of the 20th century; the first day was January 1, 1901. Centuries end with zero; they begin with one.

Without China, there might never have been a Boston Tea Party, for what the American rebels dumped into Boston harbor was a shipload of tea from Amoy, the South China port that faces Taiwan.

The telegram that William Tecumseh Sherman sent to the Republican convention of 1884 is a classic statement of unavailability. The wire stated resolutely: "I will not accept if nominated and will not serve if elected." But as a postscript to the telegram it should be noted that the convention had no serious plans to nominate Sherman in the first place.

Is one picture worth a thousand words? With a thousand words you can have the Ten Commandments, the Preamble to the Constitution, Lincoln's Gettysburg Address, the Pledge of Allegiance, the Presidential Oath, the Lord's Prayer, and have enough left over for practically the entire Bill of Rights. No sir, there isn't a picture on earth worth these thousand words.

The Hawaiian islands, discovered by Captain James Cook in 1788, are the most isolated inhabited area in the world. If you put one point of a giant compass in the middle of the island group composing our fiftieth state and describe a 2,000-mile circle, the circumference does not touch a continent in any direction.

The Supreme Court has seen 102 justices on its bench. Perhaps ten or twelve have been genuinely outstanding judges. The great bulk can be characterized simply as mediocre; fifteen or twenty have been absolute losers. William Cushing, Robert Grier, Stephen Field, and Hugo Black suffered from senility. James Wilson was a deadbeat who spent his later years dodging creditors. John Rutledge went crazy; Henry Baldwin, mentally deranged, was allowed to serve for fourteen years on the bench of the Supreme Court of the United States because its members can be impeached only for misconduct. Associate Justice Samuel Chase was loud, vulgar, and often profane.

One justice, slated to be elevated to Chief Justice, resigned due to conflict of interest when it was revealed that he was involved with a convicted swindler. James McReynolds, with a personality that can favorably be compared with that of Duke Mantee, the snarling bad guy Bogart played in *The Petrified Forest*, was an anti-Semitic volcano, regularly erupting against Louis Brandeis and Benjamin Cardozo. There never has been a period in the court's history when members were not sniping disparagingly at one another.

The discovery of America prior to the voyage of Columbus has been claimed by ten different nationalities. In addition to the Vikings from Norway, the Arabs, Basques, Chinese, Danes, Dutch, Irish, Portuguese, Italians, and the Welsh have claimed this triumph.

Spain never claimed the discovery before Columbus.

In fifteen presidential elections the candidates received less than 50 percent of the popular vote, but were successfully elected: Lincoln, Cleveland (twice), Wilson (twice), Truman, John Quincy Adams, Polk, Taylor, Buchanan, Hayes, Garfield, Benjamin Harrison, Kennedy, and Nixon.

Buffalo Bill never shot a buffalo in his life. The huge, shaggy animals that roamed the plains of North America were bison.

Annie Oakley joined *Buffalo Bill's Wild West Show* as the chief attraction. Buffalo Bill, wearing white goatee, long hair and a jimswinger coat, introduced Annie with a great flourish. She entered the arena on a galloping white horse, shooting out lit candles as she came. Her husband,

Frank Butler, would stand fifty feet from her and toss playing cards into the air, and Annie would put rifle bullets through as many as she could before they reached the floor. People in the audience would scamper for these cards, and a card with a bullet hole could be turned in at the box office for a refund of the price of admission. Because of this trick, complimentary theatre tickets, being perforated, were later called *Annie Oakleys*.

Origin of the expression "OK" is attributed to Andrew Jackson and derives from his approval of congressional legislation with an abbreviation of "Oll Kurrect." Jackson had some trouble with his grammar and spelling on occasion, but he was able to make his views understood, and he explained his philosophy on spelling this way: "It is a damn poor mind, indeed, which can't think of at least two ways to spell any words."

The earliest scandal that rocked the White House revolved around Peggy O'Neale, vivacious, flirtatious, widowed daughter of a Washington tavern keeper. In 1828 Peggy married John H. Eaton, who was soon appointed Andrew Jackson's Secretary of War. The Vice-President's wife, Floride Calhoun, a social leader, snubbed Mrs. Eaton because of her alleged intimacies. Attempts by President Jackson to insure her place in society almost disrupted the Cabinet. Vice-President Calhoun resigned.

Shortly after Eaton died in 1856, his wealthy widow married a young Italian dancing master. In quick order, the dancer went through her fortune and eloped with her granddaughter by her first marriage.

The United States stands essentially unchanged since it was federated by the thirteen colonial states. When our nation was founded, Britain was a monarchy with only symptoms of democracy, France was ruled by a king, Japan by a shogun, China by an emperor, Russia by an empress. The Holy Roman Empire embraced most of the central powers of Europe.

Germany was not in existence. Frederick the Great was gobbling up the adjoining countryside, and Prussia was becoming the most powerful state in Europe.

There was no Italy. Venice was an independent republic; Naples, Sicily, Parma, and Piacenza were governed by branches of the Spanish Bourbons; Milan, Mantua, Tuscany, and Modena were under Austrian rule, while the papal states and the Kingdom of Sardinia were under the rising House of Savoy.

Brazil belonged to Portugal, but was eventually ruled by its own monarch, the only such country in South America.

The only government among today's world powers that remains unchanged is the democracy of the United States.